CAKE DECORATING

NEW HOLLAND
PROFESSIONAL

CAKE DECORATING

RACHEL BROWN

NEW
HOLLAND

Acknowledgements
To Dawn who made sure the cakes were ready when required, Pat who has been
a great support during the photography for this book and Justine Smith for her
talent and help with the diagrams. Thank you.

First published in 2007 by New Holland Publishers (UK) Ltd
London • Cape Town • Sydney • Auckland

Garfield House
86-88 Edgware Road
London W2 2EA
United Kingdom
www.newhollandpublishers.com

80 McKenzie Street
Cape Town 8001
South Africa

Unit 1, 66 Gibbes Street
Chatswood
NSW 2067
Australia

218 Lake Road
Northcote
Auckland
New Zealand

ISBN 978 1 84537 728 1

Editor Ruth Hamilton
Designer bluegumdesigners.com
Photographer Shona Wood
Production Marion Storz
Editorial Direction Rosemary Wilkinson

10 9 8 7 6 5 4 3 2 1

Reproduction by Pica Digital PTE Ltd, Singapore
Printed and bound by Craft Print International Ltd, Singapore

contents

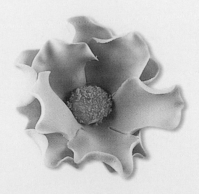

introduction

Cake decorating is an art which can be practised at different levels. This book is designed to help you improve on basic skills by taking you through several designs which use sugarpaste (rolled fondant or ready-to-roll icing), royal icing and sugar flowers. The ideas and techniques are all easy to learn and you can adapt them to suit cakes for any occasion. You don't need to be a brilliant designer; you just need a love of cake decorating to produce something really special.

I have used my years of teaching experience to write this book. I have based it on the many different courses I have taught and have tried to keep everything simple instead of getting into complicated measurements.

The sugarpaste cakes have been designed with the term "cut-out work" in mind and all the techniques are based around this. The royal icing is all geared towards piping skills; I have included basic and more advanced techniques so that you can stretch yourself as you feel ready. You will find many of the cutters have been used several times so that each one becomes a multifunctional cutter, which makes them a great investment. The cakes in both mediums gradually progress to a new level of difficulty, with extra ideas and techniques in between.

The basics of cake design never change; what changes are people's ideas of what they expect from a cake and what it is meant to represent. Don't allow yourself to be pushed into doing what you feel is beyond you, but remember it never harms to stretch yourself.

Whether you are working from home or doing a college course, I hope you will find this a helpful reference book to consult.

1 the tools

tools required for working with sugarpaste (see chapter 2)

1	Long non-stick rolling pin	6	Small sharp knife	13	Tilting turntable
2	Sugar shaker	7	Large flat dusting brush	
3	Marzipan spacers if you wish to use them	8	Crimpers	● Two pastry brushes – one for jam; one for water
4	Paste colours	9	Scribers (scalpels)	● Palette knife (metal spatula)
5	Cake smoother (flat and side smoother)	10	Sugar glue	
		11	Circle cutters	
		12	Posy picks	

tools required for working with royal icing (see chapter 3)

1 Crank-handled round-ended
  palette knife (metal spatula)
2 Metal icing rule
3 Metal side scraper

4 Turntable – a tilting one is
  really useful and is worth paying
  extra for
5 Piping (decorating) bags

- Selection of piping tubes (nozzles)
- Large flat dusting brush
- Small sharp knife
- Damp cloths – always useful
  to have to hand

tools required for making flowers with flower paste

(see chapter 4)

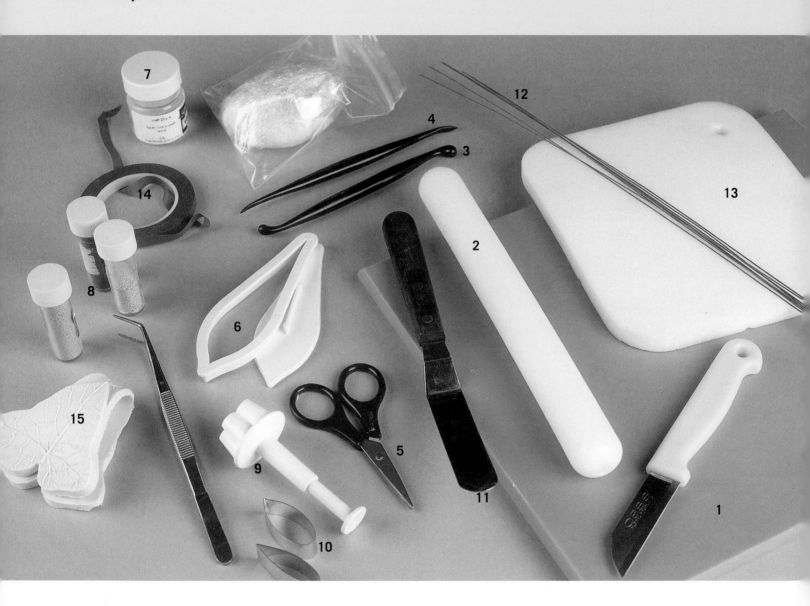

To make flowers with flower paste you do need special equipment but you will find you use the tools over and over again – making them great value for money.

1 **Non-stick rolling board** – these are available in a number of sizes and colours

2 **Non-stick rolling pin** – these are worth the money because they are so useful

3 **Balling/bone tool** – used for giving your flowers movement

4 **Veining tool** – the ideal tool for putting veins on sugar flowers

5 **Small sharp scissors**

6 **Arum lily cutter** – these come in a wide selection of sizes; several sizes are used throughout the book, but the tiny ones can be seen on page 84

7 **Sugar glue** – this can be bought ready-made or made at home

8 **Coloured semolina** – just mix food dust in with the semolina to colour it; it is so useful for so many flowers. Store in a small pot so you can use it when required; it keeps for a long time

9 **Plunger blossom cutters** – available in a few makes, but the PME range comes in a huge number of sizes

10 **Small and medium calyx cutters**

11 **Palette knife (metal spatula)** – a crank-handled (angled) one is preferable. It helps you lift your fine paste work

12 **Sugar craft wires** – they come in a variety of sizes. The higher the number, the thinner the wire. Available in greens and white.

13 **Dry flower oasis** can be purchased from any hobby store or florist. Cover it in cling film (plastic wrap) to prevent bits breaking off and getting on your cake work

14 **Florist tape** – in a number of different colours

15 **Veiner** – to give each leaf a realistic, natural look

● **Balling mat** – you place your cut-out flower shape on this to ball it

● **Non-stick small stick** – this is useful for the small delicate work

● **Daisy cutters** – there are so many on the market to choose from, all giving different effects. I use the Orchard product range, but the FMM Daisy collection set is excellent as well – it just gives finer petals

● **Plastic cocktail sticks (toothpicks)** – try to get plastic as you don't want the splinters the wooden ones may leave behind

● **Small paintbrush** for applying sugar glue

● **Large flat dusting brush**, to dust your flowers with

● **five-petal blossom cutter** – available in a vast array of sizes so you can vary the size of your work

● **Food dusts and food paste colours** – build up a collection of colours as you take on more work

● **Small amount of white vegetable fat (vegetable shortening)** – keep it in a small tub with your equipment

● **Stamens** – artificial flower stamens made from stiffened cotton come in a vast array of colours and are available from sugar craft shops

It really is worth buying good-quality metal equipment as it will give a much better result. These tools should last a lifetime if they are looked after properly. Keep them wrapped up between uses to keep them from getting scratched.

cake boards

Use a cake board that is at least 7.5cm (3in) larger than your cake to give it the best effect when finished. It is visually pleasing to ice the board and carry the design from the cake on to the board.

If you follow the collar design (see page 73), then you will need to make sure that your board is a minimum of 10cm (4in) larger than your cake. It would be terrible if you completed your cake with your collar looking beautiful, only for it to get broken as it overhangs the board.

making a piping bag

method

1 To make a piping (decorating) bag, cut some greaseproof (waxed) paper into an equilateral triangle.

2 Pick up corner C and fold it over to the dotted line, so that a sharp cone shape forms at B.

3 Wrap corner A around the cone.

4 Make sure A and C are at the back of the cone and that the point of the cone is sharp.

5 Fold points A and C inside the top edge of the bag to hold it securely. Snip off the end of B and insert a piping tube (nozzle).

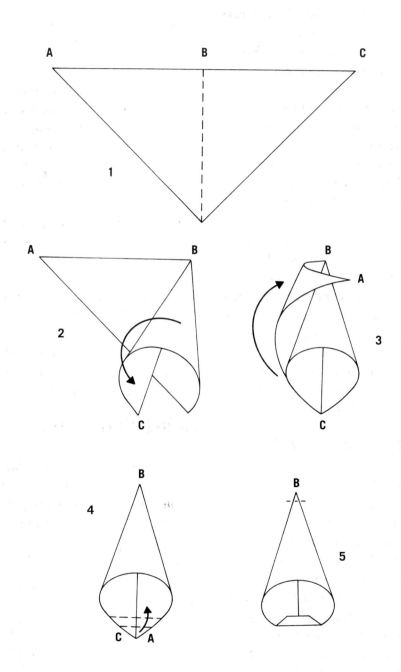

advice

- Always use a good-quality greaseproof (waxed) or parchment paper to create a good strong bag. If you use a selection of different-sized equilateral triangles and make up a quantity of piping (decorating) bags, you will always have a bag suitable for every job.

- You can buy piping bags instead of making your own. There are both reusable nylon piping bags and disposable paper piping bags available on the market. Choose whatever you find comfortable. The advantage of the reusable piping bag is that you can change the tube (nozzle) without having to empty the bag. You simply unscrew the adaptor and swap your tube. They are good for when you are piping a large area or a border. The paper bags are better for the delicate work, but go with what you feel comfortable with to achieve the best results.

inserting piping tubes

- When it comes to inserting a piping tube (nozzle), make sure that you cut only the very end off the bag (as shown in diagram 5 opposite), so that when your tube goes into the bag at least three-quarters of it is inside the bag and only one-quarter is showing. The more you have showing, the more likely it is that your bag will split when you start piping by putting pressure on the bag.

- Avoid the cheap plastic or poor-quality metal tubes as they bend and change shape so easily and do not give such a good finish. When you want to do fine delicate work, you really need a good-quality nozzle. The metal PME tubes are seamless and excellent quality, so you will find your tube will remain in perfect condition.

- When it comes to cleaning your tube, don't poke things into it to remove the icing unless it is a proper tube-cleaning brush. I leave mine in a container of water to soak the remaining icing out.

filling piping bags

- To fill the bag, hold it with the seam against your thumb and first finger so you are supporting the seam at all times – this will prevent

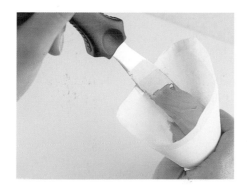

the paper bag coming undone as you fill it. Once you have your royal icing on the end of a palette knife (metal spatula), insert this into the bag and squeeze the bag together at the top.

- You will then find you can pull the knife out between your closed bag and fingers. The icing will be in the bag where you want it and not coming out all over the top.

- Once you have placed a little icing into your piping (decorating) bag, fold the top of the bag over to seal in the icing before you start piping with it. Never more than half fill your bag with icing. Overfill it and you will find that when you start piping your icing comes out of several places at the same time and you end up decorating yourself and not the cake!

2 sugarpaste

techniques

how to marzipan a fruit cake

In order to apply sugarpaste (rolled fondant or ready-to-roll icing) decoration to a cake, you will need to marzipan it first. See the chart on page 140 for the quantities you will need. It is crucial that you use enough marzipan to create a decent layer; if you put on only a very thin layer you will not end up with a good finish to the sugarpaste coating. You can use either natural white marzipan or yellow, which has colour added to it.

The kneading is a very important part of the process. You will benefit from using a good-quality marzipan as the cheapest can sometimes take much more time and effort to knead, and will still not give you a good smooth result – it will crack around the edges and corners of the cake.

I always clean my new cake boards with isopropyl alcohol (IPA), available from all good cake decorating shops. Alternatively, you can use any white alcohol, such as gin or vodka. Just splash a little on and with a piece of kitchen paper (paper towel) wipe all over the board. This removes any shop dust and will prevent the bacteria that causes mould growing between the cake and the board. If you don't have any alcohol, you could use warm, previously boiled water instead.

1 Position the cake in the centre of the cleaned cake board. If necessary fill any gaps around the base with marzipan pieces. Do not worry too much about little air holes or where fruit pieces have come out on the cake surface, but if there any larger holes just fill with marzipan. Make sure at this point that you have all the tools you require ready to use.

2 Using the correct amount of marzipan (see page 140), knead on a sugar-free surface until you have a smooth, crack-free paste. This will take quite a long time, but it's important not to rush this stage. Brush any kind of jam (jelly) all over the cake, making sure that you coat the whole surface.

3 On a light dusting of icing (confectioners') sugar, roll out your marzipan to no thinner than 8mm (3/8in), or use marzipan spacers. Try to keep your marzipan the same shape as your cake and the correct thickness. Smooth all over with your smoother tool until you cannot feel any ridges with your hand.

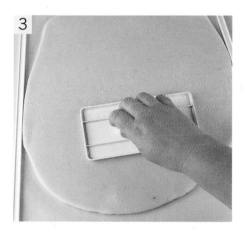

4 Place your rolling pin in the middle of your paste and lift half the paste over the rolling pin by picking it up in just two corners and flipping it over the rolling pin quickly.

5 Lift up your rolling pin and lay the edge of the marzipan against the side of the cake; flip your marzipan over the cake by rolling your pin. This

t i p

Try rolling your marzipan out on a ridged plastic sheet. There are special ones available on the market if you so wish, but any strong plastic will do. Do not use any icing (confectioners') sugar. Roll out as before, then all you have to do is turn the plastic over on the cake, peel back the plastic and proceed as before.

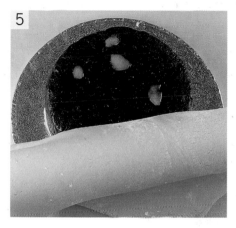

allows the marzipan to go over the cake without you having to handle it with your hands.

6 Start smoothing it out with the palm of your hand from the centre of the cake out. This is to expel any air

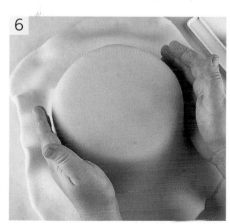

trapped beneath the marzipan. Ease the marzipan in around the sides of your cake, but use only the palms of your hands. Keep your fingertips away from the cake in order to maintain a smooth finish. You should not need to do much smoothing; just go over it lightly and finish off by going around the side of the cake with a side smoother.

7 To finish you need to trim the excess marzipan. Do not angle your knife in to the base of the cake, but keep it straight. It may look as if you are cutting too far away from the cake but that is fine. Cut a clean line (see picture). To finish just smooth round the base. Your marzipan is now totally sealed against the cake and board, and can be left at this stage to prevent your cake drying out.

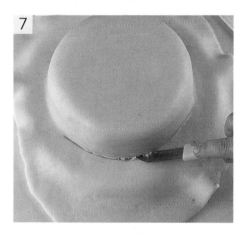

t i p

Try cutting the excess marzipan away with a pizza wheel – this gives a good clean cut – then smooth as before.

sugarpaste – preparation

Kneading sugarpaste

This is the most important stage. Remember, never knead on a surface with icing (confectioners') sugar as you will be kneading it into the paste. This will dry the paste out quicker, so it will be more likely to crack on the edges when it comes to covering the cake. You should knead your sugarpaste (rolled fondant or ready-to-roll icing) until you have a smooth, crack-free paste, which will give a good finish to your cake regardless of its shape.

Icing a cake board separate to the cake

Get everything you will need (see page 10) ready before you begin. You will also need a cup of previously boiled water. Take just enough icing to give a thin coat (see chart page 140), and roll out the sugarpaste on a very fine dusting of icing sugar. Measure to make sure it will fit over the board and smooth with the smoother. Dampen the board by brushing over some of the water. Lift up the icing over the rolling pin just as described in the marzipan section (see pages 18–19) and place it over the board. Make sure there is no air trapped underneath by smoothing from the centre outwards to expel any bubbles. Leave it to dry for about 48 hours before putting your iced cake on top. Before placing your cake on the board, put a disc of greaseproof (waxed) paper under the cake to separate the cake from the iced board. You need this greaseproof paper so that the cake and sugarpaste do not come into direct contact with each other. The fruit cake can make the sugarpaste soggy and encourage mould growth.

sugarpasting your cake

Look at the quantity chart for the icing so that you work with the correct amount of sugarpaste (rolled fondant or ready-to-roll icing) at all times. Knead it well. Once you have a good smooth ball of paste you are ready to start.

1 If you are icing a fruit cake, you need to brush it all over with gin, vodka or previously boiled water. This will moisten the marzipan so that the icing sticks to it. If you are icing a sponge cake, coat the outside of your cake with a thin layer of buttercream for the sugarpaste to stick to. Measure your cake across the top, down both sides and across the board. This will give you the overall width that your sheet of sugarpaste needs to be.

2 Roll out your sugarpaste on a small dusting of icing (confectioners') sugar, until your paste is the required size. Try to keep it in shape and keep turning it to make sure that it does not stick to the work surface. If you find as it gets larger it is difficult to turn, then just lift it by using your rolling pin to flip the icing over and if necessary sprinkle a little more icing sugar under it. Don't be afraid as you are rolling to knock your paste back into

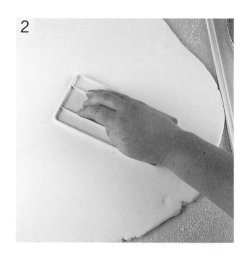

2

shape with the side of your rolling pin. You will find this also means you don't have a lot of sugarpaste left over, and thus are more likely to maintain the correct thickness to achieve a good covering. Once you have rolled out your icing, use your smoother to get rid of any ridges. When you rub your hands over it, it should feel as smooth as silk. You are now ready to cover your cake and your board if you have not iced it separately.

3 Start by laying your rolling pin across the centre of your sugarpaste. You will find it an advantage if you have a longer non-stick rolling pin and not a short wooden one. Flip your icing over your rolling pin and lift it across to your creamed cake (or, if covering a fruit cake, the moistened marzipan-covered cake).

4 If you are icing the board, then moisten the board by brushing it with a little water. Lift the icing to the cake and lay the edge of the icing against the base of the cake (or the board if you are icing that too). Start rolling your rolling pin to gently ease the icing until it lies totally over the cake. This way you do not need to use your hands and risk your fingers pressing into the icing. Starting in the centre of the cake, rub the ball of your hand in a circular movement over the top of your cake, gradually getting closer to the edge. This expels the air that is trapped between the layers. Using a smoother, gently smooth over the top very lightly. Your top is now complete.

tip

If you find you have excess sugarpaste and you know you will not be using it again for a while wrap it up in cling film (plastic wrap) and put it into a plastic bag. Put it in the freezer labelled with the date you put it in and what it is.

To ice a round or oval cake

Once you have completed the top as described on page 21, start easing the icing around the side of the cake with the palms of your hands, expelling the air as you go. Make sure the icing is lying flat over the board. You can then using a side smoother to go around your cake and the board to get a good finish. If, however, you have not yet invested in a side smoother, use your normal smoother. To finish off, use a sharp knife to trim away the excess icing from around the cake board.

To ice a square or hexagonal cake

Once you have completed the top as described on page 21, start easing the icing around the side of the cake with the palms of your hands, expelling the air as you go, but make sure you start with the corners. Pull the icing out and spread it, easing it in on the corner using the palms of your hands, not your fingers.

Once you have the icing on the corners in position, you will find the sides will just ease in. Make sure your icing is sitting flat on the board, then continue with the smoothing and trimming of the board as described above for the round cake. Any cake with corners is going to be harder to ice, but take your time, and if the icing starts to crack on the corners or edges gently rub using the ball of your hand to help iron them out. Do not use your fingers.

crimping

There is a huge range of crimpers on the market, but you will find you will keep to just a handful of the different ones as you discover your favourites. Remember to crimp as soon as you have put the icing on your cake. It is no good coming back to it several hours later because as soon as the sugarpaste (rolled fondant or ready-to-roll icing) begins to crust it is too late. Plan ahead. Have both your crimper and any template you will need if you are working on a design that is on the side of the cake ready.

Give yourself a little time to practise before you try to use a crimper directly on a cake. Roll out a piece of sugarpaste and try using the crimpers to see the different effects you can achieve with them.

The further apart the crimpers are (using the rubber o-ring to achieve this), the bigger the finished effect will be, so even with one crimper different effects can be achieved. If I am crimping onto a flat surface I hold my crimper straight up and if I am using it on the edge of a cake a 45-degree angle is better. Take your crimper and push it just a little way into the icing and squeeze it together to make the design, release the squeeze and remove the crimper. Do not dig the crimper too far into the icing otherwise you will see the cake underneath on the edge. Always remember your next crimp should be alongside the previous one, trying not to leave a gap. Continue in this manner all around the cake.

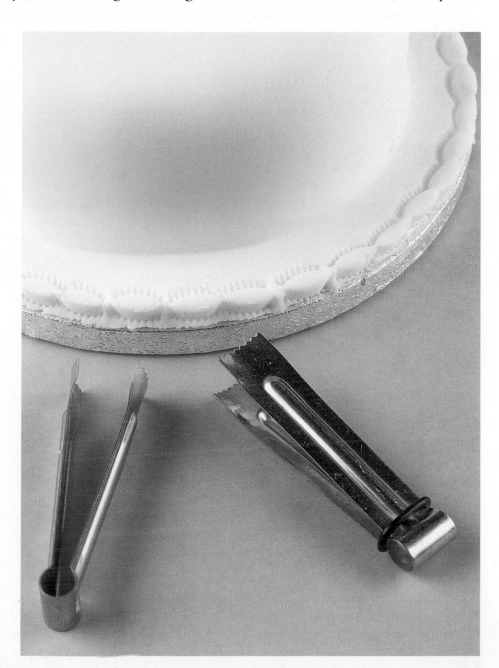

colouring sugarpaste

When you come to ice a cake remember the cake not only has to taste good but look appealing too. Avoid coating a cake in a dark colour wherever possible. A black or dark blue cake takes a lot more work to make it look tasty than a white cake with dark decorations. I have designed a white and black cake in the royal icing chapter (see page 73) but the black is not overpowering the white. The other point to remember when contemplating using dark food colours is that people could end up with a black-stained mouth, so you will find people will avoid eating the cake. There is also a stylish black and white cake in the wedding cakes chapter (see page 131).

Paste colour

From the required amount of sugarpaste (rolled fondant or ready-to-roll icing) that needs colouring, cut or pinch off a little ball-shaped piece of paste and use a cocktail stick (toothpick) to add dabs of colour (1). Knead your food colour into the paste to make a very concentrated lump of colour far darker than required (2). Once all the colour is mixed evenly in the little piece, start adding the rest of the paste a little at a time, until you have an even colour and the required shade has been reached (3). Always use concentrated paste food colours from specialist sugarcraft shops.

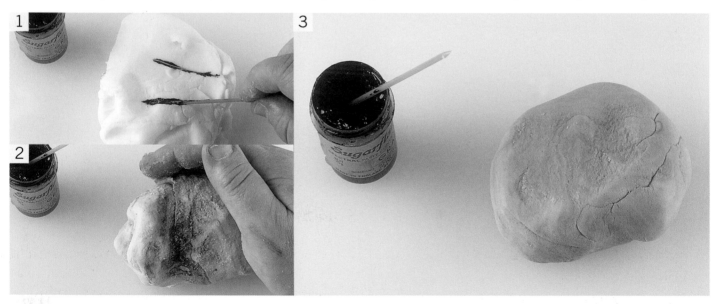

Petal dust

Never use petal dusts to colour your sugarpaste. Petal dusts are not as concentrated as paste colour (see above) and the amount of dust you would require would start drying the sugarpaste out. This would make the icing on the cake a lot more likely to crack on the edges.

Liquid food colourings

Never colour sugarpaste with the cheap liquid colours available in supermarkets. A good concentrated liquid is fine if you don't need to add too much – so they are suitable for a delicate colour. For an intense colour use a paste only.

marbling sugarpaste

Marbling sugarpaste (rolled fondant or ready-to-roll icing) can produce some wonderful patterns using the different colours to achieve the shades. I am going to give you two different methods to achieve different finishes.

Take your kneaded lump of sugarpaste, making sure that it is enough for the job you wish to do. The colours are your choice, but I think the best marbling is achieved with a white or ivory base colour.

Do not add too many colours in either of the methods of marbling as the best effects are achieved using no more than three colours. Never roll out sugarpaste on cornflour (cornstarch). This not only dries out your sugarpaste a lot quicker than icing sugar, but also has been known to start fermentation once the sugarpaste is on the cake.

Method 1

Roll your lump of sugarpaste into a simple sausage shape. Dip the tip of a knife into your chosen food colour and slice into the sugarpaste sausage across the top so it drags a little food colour through the paste. Repeat with another colour until you have inserted a little of each colour that you want to use. Fold the sugarpaste sausage in half and roll it on the work surface. Repeat this stage once more.

This method now splits into two different directions to achieve different effects. The first effect produces straight lines which are great for things like wood effects, floors etc. The second effect gives a swirl pattern, ideal in novelty cakes.

Straight lines

Start twisting the sugarpaste, as many times as you can without it splitting. Then roll it out on the work surface again, repeat at least twice more. You are now ready to roll out your sugarpaste, but remember, it must not

Straight lines

stick to the work surface as you cannot just roll it up and start again without interfering with the marble effect. You will often find the effect looks just as good if not better on the underside so you can then decide which side you wish to use.

Swirls

Once you have done the folding stages instead of twisting the sugarpaste just knead it a little. The

more you knead the more swirled and mixed the colours will be when rolled out.

Method 2

This method gives a more dramatic effect with thicker lines and bolder splashes of colour. Roll out a sausage in your base colour. Then roll out much thinner sausages of coloured paste. Wrap these around the main sausage. Do this with as many colours as you wish to use. Roll the whole sausage on the work surface and fold in half, and then proceed as in Method 1 for either straight lines or curves.

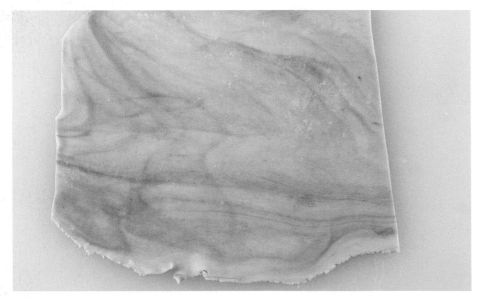

Swirls

tip

Try covering a cake in marbled paste made up of very pale tints of the same colour. This can look very delicate and because of the marbling the cake will not need too much extra decoration.

cake designs

For all these sugarpaste (rolled fondant or ready-to-roll icing) designs I have tried to keep to the theme of cut-out designs. These can be as subtle or as bright as you choose. Cut-out is simply where one layer of icing is placed on top of another, and it can produce a very effective result.

caterpillar

This is the simplest of my designs yet it is so attractive and you can make it as colourful as you want or simply work in shades of all one colour. It is an ideal cake for young children. If you are not yet happy doing any piping, this is a great cake to do as the piping required is minimal. This cake is all based on cut-out work and no other technique. Make sure that you have a good set of circle cutters for this cake.

1 This design will suit any shape and size of cake as it can be scaled up or down to suit. We have based ours on a square cake. Flat-ice your cake and the board. We have used white to coat the cake, but have iced the board separately and coated it in green for the grass. We have used a new green pan scourer to press into the icing on the board to give texture. We have left both the cake edge and the board plain to give a clean look.

3

2 Lay your cutters out to decide what size you are going to start with for the caterpillar head. Before you start working on the cake, make sure that you know what sizes you are working with. Once the circles are stuck in place, it is not so easy to pull them off and move them as it would mark the iced surface of the cake.

3 Now with your choice of sugarpaste (rolled fondant or ready-to-roll icing) colours, roll the paste out for the head of the caterpillar. This needs to be slightly thinner than the thickness you used to ice the cake. Just place the head in position on the cake; do not stick it down at this point.

tip

This design of cake could be made as a 3D novelty cake simply by using a small ball tin (pan) and making three cakes. Cut each ball in half and cover each half with a different colour for the caterpillar. Finish it off by piping on the detail.

4 Continue now with the other circles to complete the body. When you are happy with the positioning remove them one at a time. With warm, previously boiled water and a brush, moisten the cake where the circle needs to go and place it in position. Or you can use dots of royal icing – as shown in the photograph.

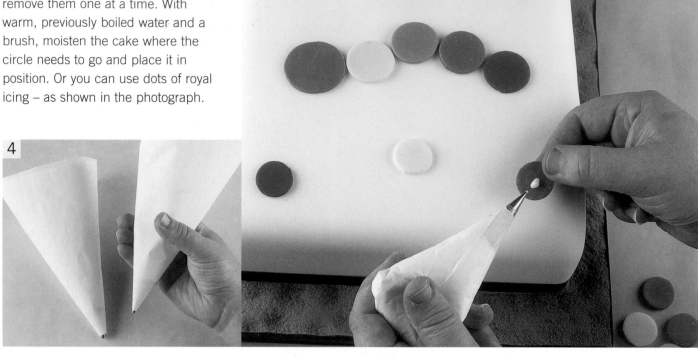

5 Now cut out a selection of smaller-sized circles from the coloured sugarpaste and place them on the cake at random, using the same method to stick them down as you did for the caterpillar. You can, if you wish, stick some smaller circles on top of the larger ones and cut out the middle of some of them if you wish to give more interest and texture.

6 Finish off the caterpillar by piping bulbs for the feet with a no. 1.5 piping tube (nozzle). The features on the face are all done using the same tube (see page 58 for piping techniques).

7 To finish off this cake, apply a ribbon to the cake board, making sure the join is at the back. Stick the ribbon on the cake; wet the ribbon and remove the excess water by running your fingers down the ribbon, then apply the ribbon to the bottom edge of the cake.

lace flower cake

This cake is a really simple, yet stunning design. It is shown here as a single tier but if you look at page 132 you will see it as a three-tier wedding cake with instructions for the modern cake top on page 116.

1 Coat a square or hexagonal cake and board: we have used white sugarpaste (rolled fondant or ready-to-roll icing), but it would look fantastic done in shades.

2 Stick a 3mm (⅛in) ribbon around the cake while the cake is still soft and freshly iced. This can be done by wetting the ribbon; remove excess moisture by running it through your fingers. You will find the ribbon will stick to the sugarpaste. Make sure that the ribbon join is at the back.

3 Choose a lace calyx cutter set or a lacy flower cutter that you would like to use. Use flower paste (see page 156 for recipe) for the side design. Work out with the cutter how many flowers you will use on each side.

4 Roll out the flower paste as fine as you can get it and cut out one flower with the cutter. Place it on a flat piece of foam to help the paste dry quickly. Carefully use a knife to lift out the centre of the petals and leave to dry. Repeat for all the flowers.

5 Once the flowers are dry, dip a brush in Tylo glue and paint around the edge of the petals. Now take an edible glitter – this can be the colour of your choice, but we have kept to white – and dust the glitter on the edges of the petals. Alternatively carefully dust the edges of the flowers with a petal dust colour, using a dusting brush, but keep this soft.

6 Moisten with water or glue around the edge of the back of the flower and just a dab in the middle, then place it in position on the cake.

7 To complete the cake I have sprinkled glitter over the surface. Dip a dry brush in the tub of edible glitter, then flick the bristles so that the glitter is sprinkled all over the cake.

frou-frou candy box

We have used candy pinks here, but this cake can be made in bright primary colours to appeal to a younger person. Here we have made this cake round, but it can be done on a hexagonal shape so that it becomes a great hatbox design.

1 We have started off by coating our cake and board all in one in a very pale candy pink.

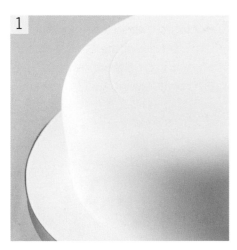

2 Leave your cake to dry. You now need to decide what colour strips you plan to use. If you are using shades of one colour, then keep to about three; if you're going funky, then have as many colours as you wish. Mix the different shades of icing so you are ready to complete this stage without having to stop to mix colours.

3 You will need a ribbon cutter to cut all the strips to the same width, keeping the strips narrow for the best effect. Mark a circle on the top of the cake as a guide for where your strips will finish.

4 Roll out only small pieces of sugarpaste (rolled fondant or ready-to-roll icing) at a time so it does not start drying out. The strips need to be placed straight onto the cake as they are cut. Before you start, you need to decide how far apart your strips will be. Make a template to mark the distance between the strips on the side of the cake. (Try cutting up a margarine-container lid, so it is washable and reusable.)

5 Attach the strips by applying a little previously boiled water to moisten the cake surface. Place

the first strip in position, then lay your template next to the strip and scribe along the template.

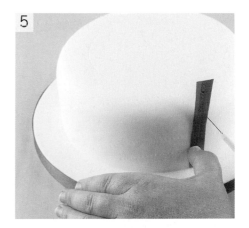

tips

- This cake is great for any age; teenagers would just adore it in bright colours.
- You need to carefully read through all steps of the instructions before you start as some stages need to be made in advance. It is not a cake that can be made in a hurry due to the drying time.

6 Now attach the second strip and continue all around the cake.

7 Next make the frou-frou bow in the centre of the cake. Cut a piece of sugarpaste about 4cm (1½in) in width and 7–10cm (3–4in) in length. The sugarpaste should not be used on its own – for about every 125g (4oz) of sugarpaste, add a teaspoon of Tylo powder, and knead it into the sugarpaste. This will help the bow set. Roll out the paste and cut with the ribbon cutter into a rectangle. Use a small rolling pin or thin bottle to wrap it around. Moisten one end with water and join the ends together. Snip the end into a V shape. Repeat so you have eight bow loops with snipped ends and eight left just folded over, making sixteen bows in total. If you cannot find anything to wrap the bow loops around, don't worry, take a piece of kitchen roll, crumple it up and use it to hold the loop in shape. At the same time, cut several bow tails. Use the same size rectangles as for the loops and cut a slanted end to each. Leave them to dry for about two days; longer if possible. I always do this stage before making the rest of the cake to give them as much drying time as possible. You can make these loops patterned with the bow cutter or leave plain.

8 All that is left to do now is to attach the bows to the cake. Attach the bow tails to the cake so that they dangle from the circle. Lay the base row of loops in a circle and attach to the cake with dabs of royal icing. The rest are positioned and held in place with royal icing to fill up the centre of the bow. They should lean on each other, or you will need to support them with foam or tissue until they are set in position. Make sure that you remove all the foam and tissue from the cake once the bows have set in position.

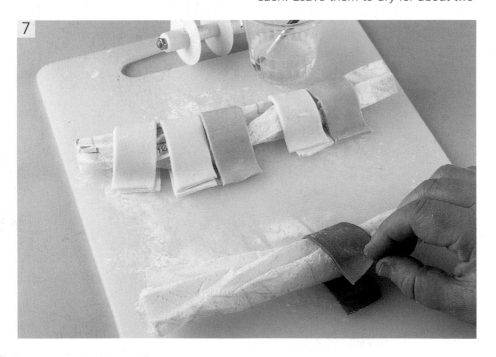

forget-me-not cake

The forget-me-not decoration can be made on either a sugarpaste (rolled fondant or ready-to-roll icing) cake or a royal-iced cake. If using the latter you may need to rethink the designs of the edges as you cannot crimp royal icing. And, unless you have a perfect edge on your royal-iced cake, you will need a little piped design. I have chosen a hexagonal cake for this as I feel this design does lend itself to a cake with corners, but the choice of shape is yours. And remember that you can get forget-me-nots in white and pink, not just blue.

1 Flat-ice your cake and board; I haven't given this cake an edge as I don't want anything detracting from the design on the cake. Leave your cake to dry for at least 24 hours before going on to the next stage.

2 Take a piece of till roll (cash register tape) or greaseproof (waxed) paper and measure round the cake.

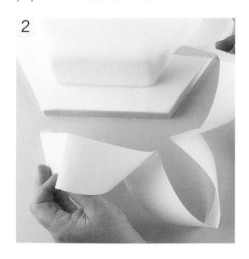

3 Fold the paper into as many sections as you have sides on your cake. (In the example shown here it will be six.) Then fold that in half again lengthways. Draw a curve across the middle of the paper, but

3

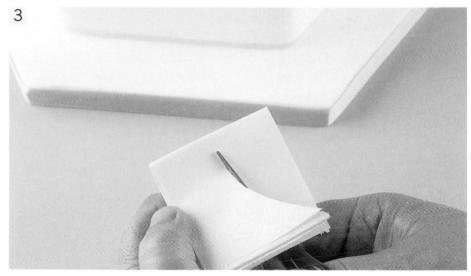

with a higher peak on one side (see photo above). Cut out.

4 Open up this paper template and place it around the cake with the high peaks on the corners of your cake and the low troughs in the middle of each side. Stick the ends together with masking tape.

5 Place your cake on a turntable and with a scriber or the point of your non-stick small stick mark lightly around the template. You may even decide that you want the sides to be

slightly more random and therefore do the side design freehand.

6 Now colour up your sugarpaste and roll it out. Press your blossom cutter into the icing and cut out the blossom. Moisten the cake where you plan to stick the icing and press the blossom directly onto the cake. If you are using a blossom cutter which does not have an ejector, then place the blossom on a piece of foam, press the middle gently so the petals raise slightly and carefully place on the cake. Using a variety of sizes of blossom cutter, work your way around the cake. You don't want to see the guideline when you have finished. I have used a yellow piped centre in all my flowers to keep the forget-me-not theme running through.

7 Pipe matching clusters of blossoms at the low troughs in the middle of each side of the cake and hanging lines of blossoms at the high peaks on the corners of the cake. Place clusters of forget-me-nots on each corner on the board.

8 I have made a cake centre to give a little height and interest, using the blossoms on stamens and larger blossoms on wires. These have been taped together with white florist tape, along with a few curled wires, and placed in a posy pick in the cake. Never just push the wires straight into the cake. I have added a few more blossoms on the same wire on just

a few of the larger stems to add effect. Once your top blossoms have dried, make sure the heads are upright and straight. Thread another dry blossom onto the wire and again hold it in position with a dot of royal icing around the wire in the centre of the blossom.

9 To finish the cake you can go around the cake piping in little delicate green leaves if you wish, but do not overdo it as you do not want the leaves to detract from the rest of the cake.

silk drape cake

This is the most complex of all the designs in this chapter to produce, but the effects are truly impressive. It introduces some advanced techniques and you will need to make two cakes. I have used a 15cm (6in) round cake and a 18cm (7in) square cake. You can go larger, or you can add another larger base cake to make a three-tier version.

1 If you are using fruit cakes, marzipan them and leave to dry. Once the top tier is dry turn it over and marzipan the base of that cake as well. If you are using sponges, then I would fill both the cakes and give them both a thin layer of sugarpaste (rolled fondant or ready-to-roll icing) first. Once the base layer or the marzipan is dry, ice your cakes in the usual manner and when they are dry turn the small cake over and ice the base. We iced our board and the base cake at the same time. You will find it an advantage to have a slightly larger cake board for this design as you will need to set the cake back on the board for the drape stage.

2 Position your top cake on the base cake and hold in place with a small amount of royal icing. Next insert two plastic dowels through both the cakes and trim the dowels off level with the top of the cakes (see the section on dowelling a wedding cake on page 127 for instructions on how to do this). Make sure you position the dowel so that the hole in the cake will be covered with the drape once it is in place. Leave the cakes to set in position.

2

tip

There are a lot of different drying times in this method so make sure you read through the whole recipe first. Plan what can be made in advance, as this design should not be rushed.

3 Roll out a large, thin length of sugarpaste. Then go over it with the silk-patterned rolling pin. This gives a great fabric effect. There is a large range of patterned rolling pins on the market, so you can use whichever you prefer.

3
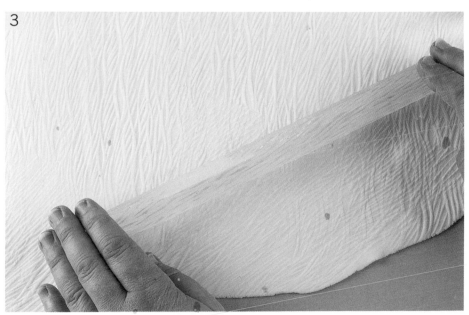

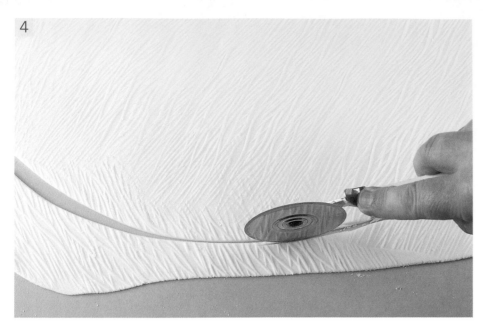

4 Cut the drape out with a sharp knife or pizza wheel. Do not make it too wide. You can always add another section if you find it hard working with a long piece in one go.

5 With warm, previously boiled water moisten the top of the cake where you want the drape to start and on the base cake so that it will hold the drape in position. Lift the drape up and get it in to position over the top of the cake so that you cannot see the join around the edges where the back icing joins the front.

6 The swag can be left plain or you can brush over it once it is dry with a shimmer dust to give it a silk effect.

7 Once the cake is dry, place a sugar flower spray on the cake. We used all autumnal colours in flowers and foliage (see chapter 5) and placed a ribbon around the board to complement the cake.

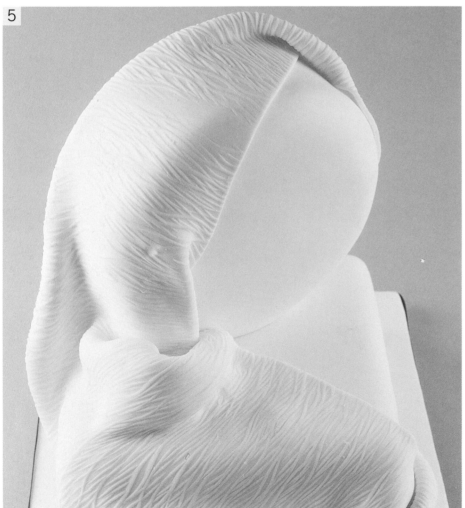

enhancements & alternatives

Here are some alternative ways of decorating the side of your cake. Garret frills are still a favourite. I will show you all stages of a basic frill, how to make a petticoat frill by layering the frills and, once you have mastered the basic frill, how to turn your cake to do the upside-down frill.

frills

1 Frills are a great way of decorating the side of a cake, but you do need a garret frill cutter which has removable middles. The sugarpaste (rolled fondant or ready-to-roll icing) must be thin. Never try to roll too much out at a time as it will dry out as you work and the frills will crack – unless you keep them under a sheet of plastic to prevent them drying out. The depth of frill depends on which centre you use – the choice is yours.

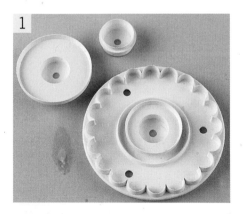

2 Once you have cut out a frill, roll a non-stick pin or cocktail stick (toothpick) over the paste. See the photo for the position of the stick and how far to roll.

3 Do not keep frilling in the one area – just roll forwards and backwards once with the stick. Move your stick along and repeat step 2 making sure you do not leave any part of the frill unrolled. It is so easy to leave a little gap between each time you roll. You will see the frill getting frillier as you continue to go around.

4 Mark with a scriber on your cake where the frill is going to go using a template. With a paintbrush moisten the line where you plan to place the frill. Cut the frill circle in one place and open it out.

5 Pick it up and starting at one end attach it to the side of the cake.

Once the frill is in position, turn the plain edges under to finish it off. Continue in this manner until you have gone all around the cake.

6 Once you have made one complete layer, repeat with a second layer, which you will see I have done

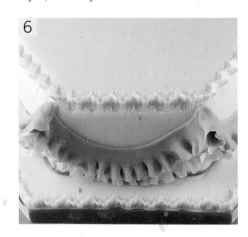

in a colour. It is necessary to raise this layer of frills about 5mm (¼in) above the first layer. Work as before, using a small paintbrush to moisten the line upon which you wish to place your frill.

7 You can continue for up to three layers. I again used the same colour icing as I had coated the cake in. This adds colour to the cake, but without it being overpowering.

8 The finishing touches to the frills can be made by piping either a small snail's trail around the top of the frill or a small dot pattern (see pages 58–9 for piped designs). Or you can leave the top of your frills plain and just finish off with the small ribbon bow at each of the points.

upside-down frills

Make sure your cake has been standing for several days to dry before applying upside-down frills.

1 Place a disc of waxed or greaseproof paper on the top of the cake, making sure it is slightly larger than the top. Place a cake drum on top of this. I always use it with the paper side against the waxed paper not the silver, just to avoid any chance of the silver side of the board coming in contact with the cake if your disc were to move. Now turn your cake over and place your cake upside down on a turntable. I like to have my cake almost at eye

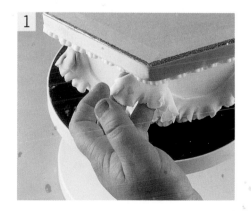

level to make it easier to see what I am doing.

2 Now treat this as if you were doing frills the usual way up, but do remember the first layer is what is seen most when the cake is turned upright again. Always turn the frill over so you are working with the back facing you as this is the side that will have some icing (confectioners') sugar on; when you turn the cake back the correct way, it is the top of the frill you will see and the side with the icing sugar will be underneath. Leave the cake upside down until the frills have had a chance to set slightly. If the sides of the cake are to have piping, do it at this stage, as it is more difficult once you have turned the cake the right way up. Carefully turn the cake back over to its normal position; the frills may turn back slightly, but this is fine.

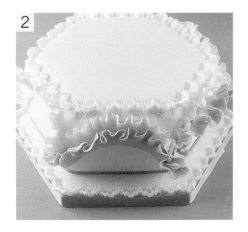

2

3 Frills done in this way give a totally different effect to a cake. Continue with your design for the top of the cake.

3

We have put together two hexagonal cakes with the frills going opposite ways to show what you can achieve by mixing designs. To separate the two cakes we have used little Perspex pots about 2.5cm (1in) high; these are petal dust containers and are available from sugarcraft shops.

top to bottom frill

Frill as normal but instead of worrying about templates you can do a top to bottom frill. This really suits a petal cake. You can purchase a straight frill cutter but this is not essential and does not give such a frilled effect as the round cutter. This frill suits a cake design that has a flower at the base of each frill.

Using the straight frill idea, try placing the frills in Vs around the cake instead of the usual curves. Do plan where your Vs start so they are spread evenly around the cake – make a template as already described on page 37. Many of the straight frill cutters also have attachments to give different effects to the top edge. You can cut little designs out of the frill at the same time as the basic frill so you don't have to pipe to finish off.

leaf-and-petal frill

Work in flower paste or sugarpaste (rolled fondant or ready-to-roll icing) for this side design. I have made my leaves in sugarpaste, but flower paste will give a finer finish. I have coated the cake in ivory and used shades of brown and orange for the leaves to make the frill and collar. The frill is made with two sizes of ivy leaves, heart leaves and rose leaves in two sizes. Lots of leaf cutters can be used to produce a different effect to a side frill. This sort of side design also looks good made with a maple leaf cutter. Have a hunt through your cutter box and experiment.

The leaves have all been given a little movement with the balling tool (see chapter 5, page 101). Layer the balled ivy leaves to produce your frill. I have put leaves together simply by laying them on top of each other and using sugar glue to stick them. I like to layer mine while they are still soft, but if you find it easier to leave them to dry first that is fine – just attach them with small dots of royal icing. This gives a more pronounced effect. This design needs to be left to dry for 24 hours. I placed a matching 3mm (⅛in) ribbon around the base of the cake, then attached a board ribbon around the cake base. On the board at the opposite end to the ribbon ends I have made a pile of leaves and a mouse hiding underneath to continue the theme of the main frill.

folded flower skirt

This just has to be one of the easiest and most effective side decorations. It is a modern design derived from what cake decorators have been doing for years. Use a large flower cutter: I like the lace flower cutters made by Orchard products as used on the cake on pages 31–2, or a calyx cutter.

1   Roll out the flower paste thinly and cut out a flower. Fold so that the top two petals of the flower fold down between the bottom three. This makes a lace piece.

2   Place a little sugar glue between the layers to keep them in place and leave to dry. I have dusted the edges

of the lace pieces. Make enough lace pieces to go all around the cake; you will not need too many as they are fairly big. Place on the cake with dots of royal icing – scribe a line where you intend to place them if it helps. Support them until they are dry by placing a piece of foam under them if you want them raised off the board or have them so that the tips sit on the

base board. This makes it even easier, as the board becomes your guideline and you do not need to worry about scribing a line onto your cake.

3   You could finish the cake off by placing a thin ribbon above the lace pieces to neaten it all off, or you could pipe a design around the cake. I have left mine plain as the white lace looks good contrasting against the lilac sugarpaste (rolled fondant or ready-to-roll icing).

4   You could even take it one stage further and, when all the lace is dry on the cake, turn the cake upside down (as described for the upside-down frill, see page 43) and place another row so that they join on to the others at the same point. This is then finished off with a small snail's trail through the centre of the joined lace pieces. Turn the cake back once you are sure the pieces are dry.

(3) royal icing

techniques

marzipan for royal icing

Marzipanning a square or hexagonal cake

This is a different method to marzipanning a cake for sugarpaste (rolled fondant or ready-to-roll icing), as you need to keep crisp, sharp edges and corners.

1   Using the marzipan guide (see page 140), select the correct quantity of marzipan for your cake.

2   Knead the marzipan on the work surface – without icing (confectioners') sugar – until you have a smooth, crack-free paste.

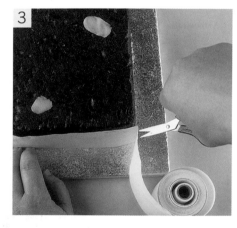

3   Measure the sides and depth of your cake with a plastic measure or with a till roll (cash register tape). (This is very handy as it is disposable and you can cut it to just the correct length so you have a good template to work with.)

4   Prepare your cake as in the marzipanning for sugarpaste (see page 18), filling in the fruit holes and packing the bottom if necessary, then spread jam (jelly) just over the sides of the cake.

5   Roll the marzipan into a sausage shape with your hands.

6   Dust the work surface with a light sprinkling of icing sugar. Then roll out the marzipan sausage with your rolling pin and flatten it until you have a thickness of 8mm (³/₈in). Use marzipan spacers if needed, as they will guarantee your marzipan will be of an equal depth. With your smoother, smooth over the marzipan until it feels smooth and ridge-free.

7   Using the template made in step 3 above, cut a rectangle to fit the first side of your cake. I always use a pizza wheel to cut the marzipan because you don't get the drag that you get with a knife. Place the marzipan against the side

7

and place it over the top of the cake. Smooth it over and trim away any excess with a small sharp knife. Re-smooth if necessary to keep crisp edges.

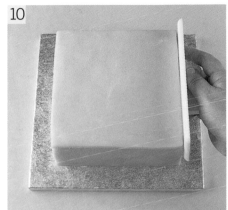

10

of the cake. You may find you need to go over it again with your smoother. Trim any excess with a small sharp knife.

8   Cut a second piece of marzipan for the next side of the cake. With warm, previously boiled water and using a clean brush moisten down the edge of the piece of marzipan already on the cake. This will be the starting point for you to attach the second piece of marzipan against the cake. Keep a sharp crisp corner.

9   Roll and cut the marzipan as before. Repeat the process on all four (or six) sides of your cake. Go over all the sides with your smoother until you feel you have a good seal on the corners.

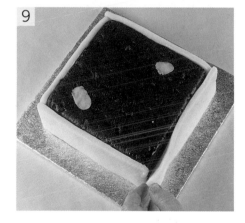

9

10   Now take the remaining marzipan and knead it back into a ball. On a lightly dusted surface roll the marzipan out into the same size and shape as the top of your cake. Remember to re-measure the top as it is now slightly larger. Use your rolling pin to knock the marzipan back into shape as required. Cut your marzipan to the required size. Moisten all around the top edge of the marzipan

11   If you find your edges are not quite sharp enough, place one smoother against the side of the cake and another smoother on the top. Move the top one by applying a little pressure on it in order to butt it up to the smoother at the side. This will move just enough marzipan to give you a crisp edge.

Marzipanning a round or oval cake

1 Prepare your cake as in marzipanning for sugarpaste, filling in the fruit holes and packing the bottom if necessary. Use jam (jelly) on only the sides of the cake.

2 Knead your marzipan as for the square cake (see page 50) and roll your marzipan into a sausage.

3 Dust the work surface lightly with icing sugar and roll the sausage out with your rolling pin to a thickness of 8mm (³⁄₈in). As in step 3 for marzipanning a square cake (see page 50) create your template for the sides to measure the whole circumference of the cake. Cut your piece of marzipan with about an extra 2.5cm (1in) added to the circumference length. Roll up the strip of marzipan to make it easier to handle but be careful not to squash it with your fingers.

4 Place your cake on a turntable. Place the marzipan roll against the side of the cake and unroll it as you turn the cake round. Let the marzipan overlap and then with a small sharp knife cut a straight line going through both layers of overlapped marzipan. Remove the excess marzipan; slightly moisten the edges of the marzipan so that both ends meet perfectly. Now go round the side with your smoother, and trim the top edge if required and smooth. Make a

template of the top of the cake. Roll and cut out a piece of marzipan to the size of the template. Place on the cake, following the instructions on page 51 for the square cake.

Drying the marzipan

Now leave your marzipan to dry for at least four days. Your cake is totally airtight with the marzipan so the cake will not dry out. Do not put your cake in an airtight container as this will prevent the marzipan drying out. It is best placed in a cake box, to keep it dust-free, in a dry place. Never leave it in an atmosphere that can be steamy or moist, such as the kitchen.

tip
Why do we marzipan the sides first and not the top?

I have always found that when you come to icing your cake – particularly the stage when applying pressure with an icing ruler – if you have marzipanned the top first it is easier to accidentally open the seam where the marzipan joins on the sides. Opening this seam lets royal icing into the seam so you are much more likely to discolour the icing, which you really want to avoid. However, there is no hard and fast rule about this; a lot of people do the top first, then the sides, so go with what you find easier.

colouring royal icing

Keep the colours in royal icing soft because they are much more pleasing to the eye. Strong colours tend to dominate and you will lose the effect of the delicate work you have done. Every time you scrape the edges of royal icing with a knife you will find the area will become white and this will be far more obvious on a stronger colour.

Liquid food colour

Never use liquid food colours as they will change the consistency of your royal icing.

Paste food colours

Paste food colours are good, but they do contain glycerine. This is fine in the coating, but is more difficult to use with some of the decorating techniques described later. If you are using paste remember how strong the colours are. Just put the tip of a cocktail stick (toothpick) into the pot to get the colour. Mix enough royal icing all in one go for your requirements as you will never be able to mix the exact same shade again.

Petal dusts

These are mainly used to add colour with a brush. They give a very soft colour, however, so they are ideal for adding a tint to your royal icing. You must make sure you mix all the grains in thoroughly with a wooden spoon or plastic spatula so that you have an even mix. Otherwise you may end up with dark blobs in the finished cake, which will totally spoil the effect you have spent time working to achieve.

using royal icing

Always make up a large batch of royal icing and keep it in an airtight container. Try to make enough icing in one go to complete the whole cake. Make the royal icing at least 24 hours before you wish to start coating the cake and make sure all your tools are clean and grease-free before you begin mixing. It is a good idea to stir your icing each day to keep it at its best and never use icing straight out of the pot before you have beaten it.

Royal icing needs to be thick enough to form a soft peak. Once you have mixed the icing, stir it with a wooden spoon – you want the peaks to just hold with only the top of the peaks flopping over and not holding stiff. Always stir with a plastic spatula or wooden spoon as opposed to a metal one. A metal spoon will break down the air while stirring and can dirty the icing.

When applying royal icing, do not leave it too long between coats. Otherwise you find the layers do not adhere to each other. When you come to cut the cake, the icing then shatters into shards of icing instead of remaining together.

Royal icing dries very hard, which can make it difficult to cut. To prevent this add the glycerine that is recommended in the royal icing recipe (see page 154). This will make it far easier to cut without the use of a hammer and chisel.

tips

● Make your royal icing at least 24 hours before you want to start icing your cake.
● Stir your icing every day to keep it in a far better condition and stop it separating.

how to royal-ice a cake

Coat one – the top

1 Place your cake on a turntable. Take your stirred royal icing and spread it on to the top of your cake using a palette knife (metal spatula). Once you have put rough icing all over the top of your cake, place your palette knife with the tip in the centre of your cake and paddle (rock) it backwards and forwards, working your way all around the cake. This breaks down any trapped air – you are not trying to smooth the icing.

2 Remove your cake from the turntable – never try to ice on the turntable as the cake will keep moving around, which is not helpful at this stage. Place it on one of your damp cloths or on a piece of non-slip matting to prevent the cake slipping around while you work on it.

3 Using the second clean damp cloth, wipe your metal ruler just before you start. Start at the side nearest you on a square cake and at the nearest point to you on a round cake. Using the rocking movement that you have already used in step 1, paddle your way across the top of the cake with your metal ruler, keeping a good even pressure. When you get to the other side of the cake pull the rule towards you in a swift movement, keeping an even pressure and making sure you keep your ruler at a 45-degree angle. At this stage don't worry about any icing that has gone down the sides of the cake. If you are happy with the coat, then leave it. If it has lots of air bubbles, repeat the process. Don't worry if you feel you can still see some of the marzipan through it; think of this first coat as only a filler coat.

4 When you are happy with your coat, place your cake back on the turntable and with your side scraper go around the edge of the cake to clean up the sides and to give a good clean edge to your cake. It is very important you clean up after every stage. Now leave this to dry for at least 12 hours.

5 Once the top has dried, take a small sharp knife and if necessary go around the edge and scrape off any excess icing that may interfere with the side coats. Make sure that you dust off any fragments of loose icing; a good dusting brush is really helpful for this.

Coat one – the sides of a square cake

6 Place your cake on the turntable and have your side scraper and damp cloth to hand. Using your crank-handled (angled) palette knife, apply previously stirred royal icing to cover the side of the cake. Still using your palette knife, paddle the icing as you did on the top of the cake (see above).

7 Take a metal side scraper and wipe your damp cloth over it. Hold the scraper so that your fingers are evenly spread out, then place your scraper just beyond the side of the cake you are working on. This ensures you get the side smooth right from the edge of the side. You need to hold your side

7

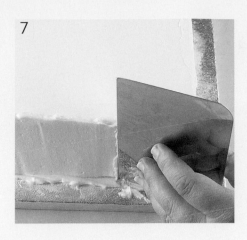

scraper at a 45-degree angle. Remembering to apply even pressure at all times, pull the scraper across the side of the cake. Work quickly to achieve a smooth result.

8 When you are happy with the side, run your side scraper along the top of the cake keeping it horizontal, that is, at the same angle as the surface of the top – do not angle it down. Repeat the process down both uniced sides to clean up the edges and to keep your corners crisp.

8

9 Scrape any excess off the board to clean up the base of the cake.

9

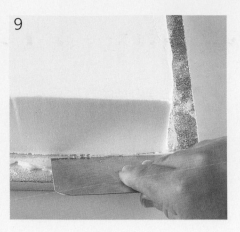

Repeat the whole process on the opposite side, and the cleaning down afterwards. Then leave it to dry for at least 12 hours.

10 Once the first two sides are dry, repeat the whole process on the opposite two sides and leave them to dry again for at least 12 hours.

Coat one – the sides of a round or oval cake

11 Place your cake on a turntable. Paddle your icing all around the cake, then go round again, paddling out the air bubbles.

12 Wipe the side scraper with a damp cloth. Starting as far round the back as you can reach, almost like cuddling the cake, hold the side scraper at a 45-degree angle and pull the scraper round the cake as you turn your turntable. Finish off at the point where you started. Never let your scraper tilt to a 90-degree angle: the finish will not be as good and you may end up with little lines going

round your cake. It is also much harder to keep an even pressure at 90 degrees.

12

Coats two and three

Now your cake – whether square or round – has had its first coat. After each coat remember to clean down with a little sharp knife and dust away excess bits. Repeat the whole process – to the top and the sides – at least another two times, or until you are happy with the cake.

Achieving a textured finish

You can now buy side scrapers which create lines around the cake, giving you instant decoration. These are used only on the final coat. They are made of a hard plastic instead of metal, but for a decorative coat they work well. Treat them just like the side scraper you have been using on the previous layers. Take your time before you do this layer on your cake and practise on a board to see which design you like the best. On page 63 you will also find a design making use of a stippled–texture effect.

troubleshooting

Uneven pressure

When flat icing the top of your cake, if you apply more pressure on at the beginning and/or end of each coat you may find your top looks a little sloped or humped. To ensure this does not happen, start on a different side (with a square cake) or at a different point (on a round cake) with each layer you apply. This will ensure that the cake will end up flat overall.

When concentrating on getting a smooth result to the sides of your cake, you may forget to maintain even pressure. If you apply more pressure at the top of the scraper you will find your cake will begin to get a "chimney" effect. This means your cake would be wider at the base than the top. If you place too much pressure on the base of the scraper then you get a "funnel" effect, so it is wider at the top than the base. Both can be corrected.

■ If your cake has got the chimney effect, then paddle a thick layer of icing around the top three-quarters of the sides of the cake. Wipe your side scraper with a damp cloth. Then, using your scraper at a 45 degree angle, go all the way round the side on a round cake, or along each side on a square cake. Don't expect this coat to be perfect – it is only a correction coat. Tidy up the top edges of the cake and leave it to dry for at least 12 hours.

■ Tidy up your cake with a sharp knife and dust off any royal icing dust, then continue icing in the normal way. Although this correction will mean your icing is a little on the thicker side, it will correct the shape. And it's easier and cheaper than stripping off the marzipan and icing and starting all over again.

■ If your cake has the funnel effect then paddle icing on to the bottom three-quarters of the sides and proceed as described above.

icing the cake board

Once your cake is dry you can ice your board. There are two possible methods and both work well.

Method 1

1 Spread royal icing around the cake board using as little icing as possible because you don't want it to go up the side of the cake.

2 Wipe your side scraper with a damp cloth. Holding it at a 45 degree angle to the board, go around the

2

board just as you did when icing the cake. If you are doing a square cake, you may find that this is a little more difficult and takes a bit more practice.

3 You will need at least two coats to get a good finish.

Method 2

4 Place some royal icing into a small bowl. Using a water dropper or teaspoon, add droplets of cold water or liquid albumen. (Liquid albumen – albumen mixed with water – should give a shinier finish.) Be careful if using a teaspoon as it is easy to put in too much. Gradually mix in the droplets using a wooden spoon or plastic spatula until you have the consistency of thick double cream. Once stirred the icing should go smooth by the time you have counted to ten. So stir and count. If it is smooth at eight seconds, it's too thin and needs a little more royal icing added to thicken it. Working with icing that's

too thin can result in a runny mess and a bumpy surface once the icing has dried. But if it is of the correct consistency, the board will have a beautiful finish. Cover the bowl with a damp cloth to prevent the icing crusting until you are ready to use it.

5 Place your cake on the turntable and take a ready-made piping (decorating) bag (see pages 14–15). Tip your icing into the bag, which does not require a tube (nozzle). Half fill the bag and turn the top over to seal the icing in. You want only a tiny hole in the end of the bag; you may find you do not even need to

cut anything off the end of the bag as you want nothing larger than a pinhead. This is so that, as you squeeze the icing through the bag, you burst the air bubbles in your icing as you go; this should give a good finish to your board.

6 Start squeezing the icing onto the board and cover a section of about 5cm (2in). Then do 5cm (2in) to the left of it and 5cm (2in) to the right, and continue all around the cake board. This prevents the icing having time to start crusting and a start line showing. If you need to help the icing to cover each small area, or to get it into a corner, use a small clean paintbrush in a circular movement to move the icing.

7 Place an angle-poise desk lamp near the board if you have one. The heat from the lamp will crust the icing more quickly. This will prevent any air bubbles that may have escaped rising to the surface and ruining the smooth finish. Leave the board to dry for 24 to 48 hours before starting to pipe decorations on your cake. The icing should dry with more of a shine on it.

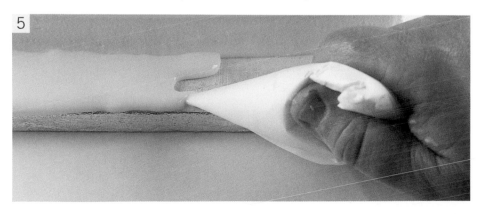
5

- Stir your icing every day; this keeps it in a better condition and stops it separating.
- If you do have to mix a second batch, make sure that you make it with the same albumen. If you start with egg white keep to it and to the same type of egg. A hen egg which has been fed on corn produces a much yellower icing than that made with albumen substitute, which will give a beautiful white icing. Never mix the two. Both look great on their own, but the difference will show if you mix them.
- Have all your tools ready to use before you start, as royal icing starts drying out as soon as you start working with it.
- Hold your icing ruler between your thumb and fingers. Practise rocking your ruler so that when you come to ice your cake you know how to do it in such a way that you get icing on only the one side of the ruler. You rock the ruler from your wrist. Do not turn the ruler – let your wrists do the work. Once you master this technique, the icing of a cake will become much easier.
- If you want a coloured coat, mix enough icing to coat the whole cake several times over. I would recommend you do the first coat in white as a filler coat, before going over with coloured coats.
- Never leave your cake in a kitchen or any damp room. Royal icing will absorb any moisture, with devastating results.
- When you are working with royal icing, never let water droplets get near the cake. Any water splashes on the cake will eat into the icing and create a hole. If you do have an accident, rub some icing (confectioners') sugar onto the cake as soon as it happens to dry the spot on the cake out. Once it has dried, you can then try to disguise the defect.

piping

See pages 14–15 for details on making a piping (decorating) bag.

Shells

Holding your bag at a 45-degree angle, position the piping tube (nozzle) on a covered cake. Squeeze the bag so the royal icing emerges all round the piping tube. Squeeze the icing out to the size of shell required, then drag the piping tube to produce a tail to complete the shell. As you drag your tube, release the pressure on the bag. Start the next shell on the tail of the previous shell, making sure that you keep them all equal size.

Fleur-de-lis

This uses the same method as for piping shells, above. The difference is that you do only the first shell straight. The second shell is piped just to the left of the first one, starting halfway down it and with its tail curving down towards the bottom of the first shell. The next shell is done in the same way, although it starts halfway down the right side of the second shell. Repeat as many times as necessary. You can use a variety of tubes from a no. 5 or no. 6 shell tube to a plain no. 3 tube.

Upside-down shells

This is a simple design for the bottom of a cake. Each shell is piped individually. Hold your piping tube at the base of the cake and squeeze as for a shell, but this time the tail needs to go up the side of the cake. It is

important that all the tails finish at the same height. This design can be taken a stage further with small piped loops hanging between them from the tip of one shell to the other.

Scrolls

Holding the piping bag at a 45-degree angle, position the shell piping tube on the covered cake or board, and pipe outwards in a circular movement. Move into an S shape and release the pressure on the piping bag to break off the icing. Repeat, overlapping the scrolls slightly and keeping them all the same size. A plain no. 3 or 4 tube gives a good effect for a smaller version of the scrolls. See the royal-iced black-and-white cake on page 73.

Snail's trail

The only difference between this technique and piping shells is that it is done with a much smaller plain writing tube. Use a no. 1, 1.5 or 2 tube. It is excellent as a finishing touch in a small area.

Bulbs

This is a simple piping design, but it can take a little practice to get all the bulbs even. Hold your piping tube vertically on a covered cake or board, and squeeze until your bulb is the required size. Release the pressure on the bag at this point and pull out the

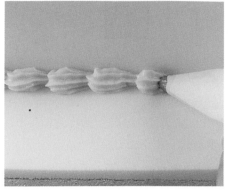

Shells

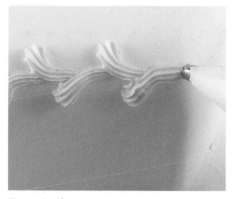

Fleur-de-lis

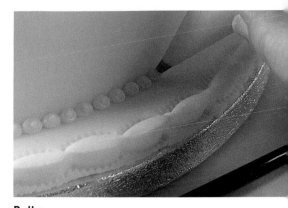

Bulbs

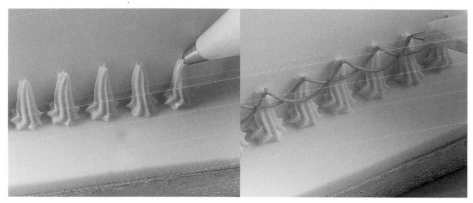

Upside down shells

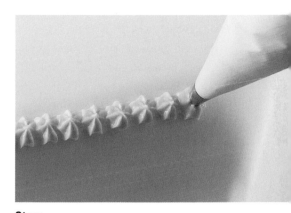

Stars

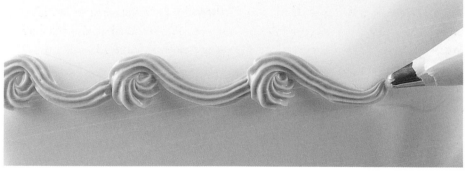

Scrolls

tube from the bulb. If you find you end up leaving a little peak on each bulb, dab the peak down immediately with a damp paintbrush. If you find it easier, pipe the bulbs onto a plastic wallet or sleeve. When they are dry, you can lift them off the plastic and position them on the cake. This way you choose only the best and those that are all the same size. Once you have mastered bulbs you can use different-sized bulbs in your cake design, which look very delicate.

Stars

Follow the same principle as explained for bulbs, but use a no.5 or 6 star tube instead of a plain writing tube.

Snail's trail

Straight lines

Holding the piping bag vertically, position the piping tube on a covered cake or board. Lift the piping tube, at the same time applying pressure on the piping bag. Never apply pressure until you are ready to start the line, and do not drag the piping tube across the cake or board. By lifting it, you will gain more control over your piping and will be able to see where you need to "land" to finish the line. Just before you finish the line, release the pressure on the piping bag so that you can complete the line in your own time.

Trellis

This is a continuation of the straight-lines technique, but this time it covers a whole area. Pipe a series of straight lines going one way, then pipe another series on top going the opposite way. Try to keep even spacing between the lines. It can take a long time to pipe trellis, so do it in sections; you will then find it easier to stop and start.

Basket weave

You will need to prepare two piping bags for this, one with a plain no. 4 tube and the other with a basket-weave piping tube. Start at the back of your cake and with the plain-tubed bag pipe a vertical line down the cake. Next take the basket-weave-tubed bag and pipe a horizontal line about 2.5cm (1in) long going across the vertical line at 90 degrees. Repeat this process going down your cake, leaving a piping tube width between each line of basket weave that you pipe. Now pipe another vertical line

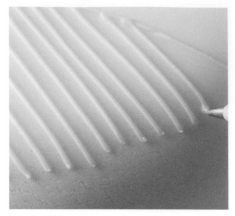
Straight lines

Basketweave

Three-line grade work

down your cake with the plain piping tube so that it sits along the ends of your lines of basket weave. Now with the basket-weave piping tube, start from the first plain line you piped

Trellis

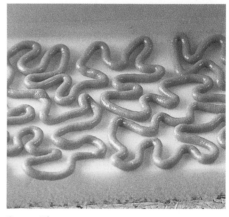
Cornellie

down and pipe a horizontal line between the previous lines and crossing the second plain line, keeping the spacing even. Continue like this around your cake until you meet up at the beginning.

Cornelli

This is one of the hardest piping designs to achieve. Some people compare it to S and C shapes; others to Ms and Ws. Use a no. 1 tube and start piping a wavy, squiggly line in a completely random fashion so you cannot see where the line is going to travel to next. You can stop and restart when needed; use a damp paintbrush to get rid of any join marks if you make one when you resume piping. The lines should be kept with even spacing and should not touch anywhere.

Three-line grade work

This is simpler than it sounds. Make up three piping bags, one with a no. 2 tube, one with a no. 1.5 and the third with a no. 1 tube. Label which bag is which. The three lines need to be as close to each other as you can get without them touching. You will see they gradually step down. If you find three-line grade work hard to do, try just doing two-line grade work to start with.

Lace work

Piped lace work makes the ideal edging for covered cakes or boards. It looks fragile, but when it is made correctly it is robust and can easily survive being transported. Just make sure that your royal icing recipe does not contain liquid glucose, which prevents it from setting too hard (see recipe, page 154).

Before you begin, you will need to create a template and transfer it to a cake covered at least 24 hours previously. Go through your lace collection to find a pattern you like, then trace or draw it onto a piece of plain paper. See page 158 for a small selection of simple lace patterns. If the pattern is small, it makes sense to repeat it several times on the paper, so that once you start piping you can continue without any interruptions.

Place the paper inside a plastic sleeve or wallet, which you can find at any office-supply shop, and secure it to a firm surface with masking tape.

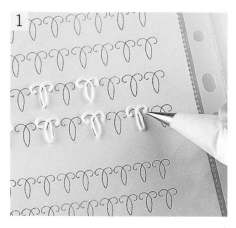

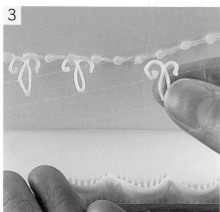

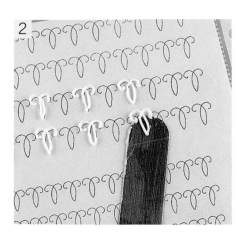

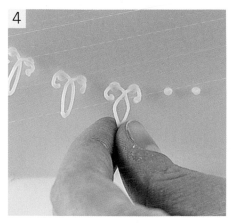

You will be piping directly over the design and do not want it to slip or shift. Coat the plastic sleeve with a thin layer of vegetable fat (shortening). This will prevent the lace work from sticking and breaking when you try to lift it.

1 Using a plain writing tube, pipe over the design. Keep the piping tube close to the surface of the plastic sleeve and try to keep the pressure even.

2 All of the lines of a "lace" motif should touch to prevent your work from falling apart when you lift it. Pipe more pieces than you actually need in case of mishaps. Leave your work in a

warm place to dry. When it is ready, run a palette knife (metal spatula) beneath each piece of lace work to release it from the plastic sleeve.

3 To attach the lace work to the cake, pipe a small, neat snail's trail of royal icing along the outline that you traced on the cake or board's covering. Gently push the pieces of lace work into the line of royal icing.

4 Alternatively, pipe two tiny dots where each piece of lace work is to be placed, and gently push the pieces on top of the dots. If you use this technique, make sure that the pairs of dots are evenly spaced.

cake designs

The four royal-iced designs on the following pages gradually get harder and introduce new skills. Do not get out your depth before you are ready; often the simplest of designs can look the most effective.

stipple cake

This is the simplest of the four designs: it does not require much piping so it means you can still create a beautiful cake before you have fully mastered your piping skills. The texture still makes it interesting, and it is suitable for a square cake. The main tools needed are masking tape and a sponge. Masking tape will adhere to the cake without marking it, and it peels off easily.

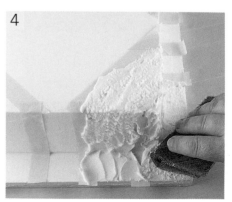

1 Royal-ice a square cake to a good finish, followed by the board, and leave them to dry. Make a triangle template to fit the corner of your cake. You need only one. With your scriber, scribe a line along the paper template. Repeat on all four corners.

2 Next measure about 1–2.5cm (1/2–1in) in from a corner along both sides, and mark these points with your scriber. Using a ruler, scribe a line to join these marks up, and attach a piece of masking tape to run along these lines. Now with a ruler mark a vertical line from the taped lines down the side of the cake and carry these lines across the cake

board. Repeat this process to create a second band of masking tape further in from each of the four corners. Again place masking tape on them all.

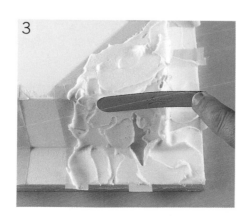

3 With a palette knife (metal spatula), spread a thin layer of royal icing in between the masking-taped lines. You are not trying to get it smooth, but keep the icing thin.

4 Take a new sponge and dab over the royal icing. Don't worry if it goes on the masking tape. Repeat on all four sides and on the board as well. You may find it easier to work on a turntable for this and have it tilted for the sides. Now repeat the process on each corner.

5 When you have completed all the sides remove the masking tape. Make sure you pull the tape off in a straight line and not at an angle.

6 Now complete the rest of the cake with some simple piping. Pipe around the base of the cake just on the sides between the textured

5a

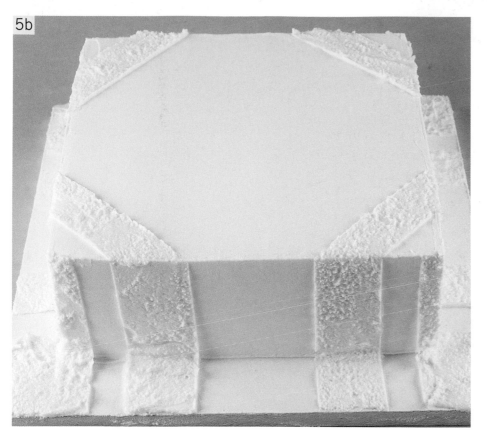

5b

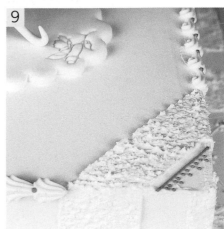

9

panels. I have piped a small shell using a PME no. 5 tube (nozzle). Repeat around the top of the cake.

7 In the middle of each side choose a simple design, perhaps one of the two shown right. You can trace these to make your own templates. Fix your template to the cake with masking tape and scribe the design on the side.

8 With a PME no. 1.5 tube, pipe the design on the cake over your scribing. (Practise on a flat board first.) I am keeping all my design white at this stage; when the decoration is finished I will go back and overpipe with a colour if required.

9 Mirror-image the side design onto the board to carry the theme through. Now go back and add colour if you wish to do so. I overpiped the central dots on the side design, and a small dot at the base of each in colour. On each corner I piped a straight line and a three-dot pattern. This has lifted the whole cake design.

10 To complete this cake you need to add a name, monograms or chosen cake top. I have used my completed parasol cake top, which I have mounted on a sugar plaque so that it can be taken off and kept afterwards (see page 122).

Side design 1

This design is a simple curve line with decoration in the middle and at each end. This is formed by a central bulb with four smaller bulbs around it. (See page 58 for how to pipe bulbs.)

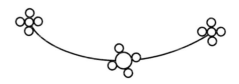

Side design 2

This is slightly more difficult. It is a curved S shape dotted with lots of bulbs, which are ringed with tiny bulbs, spaced along the line. Each tiny bulb or "petal" is then pulled out to a little point with a damp paintbrush. Try to put the same number of petals around each central bulb.

daisy-chain cake

The sides of this cake incorporate simple unwired daisies that are complemented by the small wired arrangement on the top. The daisies will need to have been made and left to dry while you are decorating the cake. See page 87 for how to make the daisies.

1 This design looks great on any shaped cake; I chose to keep mine to a simple round cake. Flat-ice your cake and the board. Measure round the side of your cake with a piece of till roll (cash register tape) or greaseproof (waxed) paper which represents the depth of your cake. Decide how often you want a daisy to appear and fold your paper this number of times. I like the chain effect, so I have not spread mine out too much. On your folded template draw a curved line, and cut along this with scissors.

2 Pipe around the base of your cake with a small dainty shell using a no. 5 tube (nozzle). Around the top I have used the fleur-de-lis design as you don't want a design that is too heavy and does not complement the rest of the cake. Pipe the fleur-de-lis with a no. 5 tube.

3 Place your template around the cake and join with masking tape. Place your cake on a turntable and with a scriber or the point of a non-stick small stick, mark the curved line lightly around the template.

4 Insert a no. 1.5 tube in a piping (decorating) bag, and fill with pale-green icing. Practise piping this design on a flat board first, as it is harder to do on the side of your cake.

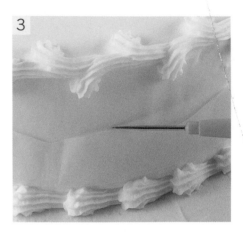

You don't need to pipe the line all in one go. Try to stop where you know you will be putting a daisy flower head as this will hide your joins.

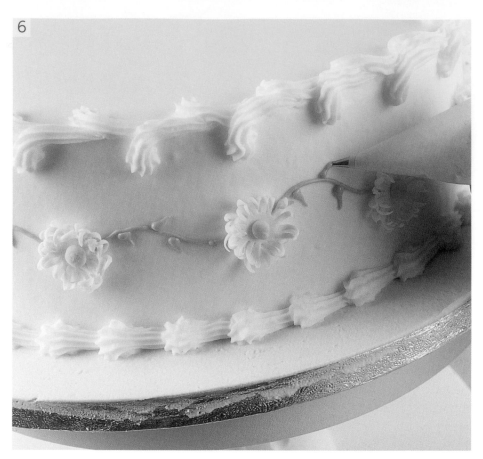

Pipe the line all around the cake and leave to dry.

5 With your cake still on the turntable, attach the daisies you have made by sticking with a dot of royal icing. I always use the same colour as my piped line so, in this case, pale green.

6 Pipe a few leaves onto the green line between the daisies, by using a no. 1.5 or no. 2 tube to pipe a single snail's trail from the line.

7 Now you can place the daisies on the board, but they need to be positioned so they sit between the daisies on the side of the cake. For the cake top, see page 108.

tip
Tilt your cake to make applying this wavy line around the side easier. If you don't have a tilting turntable, try resting the cake against a bowl with a damp cloth over it to prevent it slipping.

elegance cake

This should improve your piping skills. Much of the design is based on different sizes of bulbs and dots. You will also be learning a simplified version of oriental string work. I have coated a long octagonal cake with marzipan and royal icing, but the design can be applied to any cake with straight sides.

1 Take your time to get your templates correct for this cake. Make a template to sit on the top of the cake in a diamond or square shape.

2 Start by scribing what will be the outer line on the top of the cake. You will not need to scribe the inner lines as you will find you can follow the outer line as a guide.

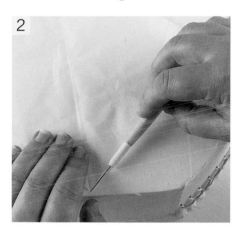

3 Fill four piping (decorating) bags, three with white icing and one with orange. All should be piped in white, except for the final line, which is piped in orange. Pipe the outside line with a no. 2 tube (nozzle) and the next inner line with a no. 1.5 tube.

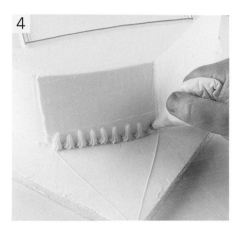

Overpipe the no. 2 line with a no. 1.5 tube. With a no. 1 tube, pipe the innermost line, then overpipe the middle no. 1.5 line and the outer no. 2 line. The outer line is now three lines deep, the middle two lines deep and the inner just one line deep.

4 On the four equal-sized sides of the cake, pipe upside-down shells

around the bottom edge of each side. (See the piping instructions for this on page 58.) Keep your shells all the same size and even. Leave to dry.

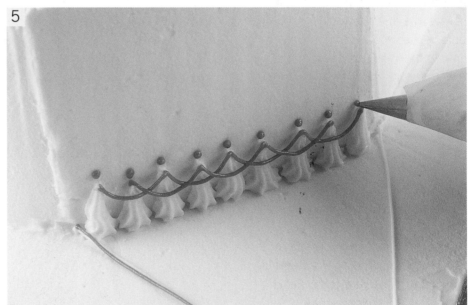

5 Starting at the top of one of the shells, pipe a curved loop – just as in the piping instructions on page 58 – using a no. 1 tube and finish the loop at the top of the next shell but one. Keep piping the curved loops so they go from the top of one shell to the top of every other shell. You may find it easier to pipe a few and leave them to dry for a few minutes before doing some more. If one loop breaks it will not affect anything else. When you have completed one row go back and do a second row in between the first row. Don't do this unless you feel confident with the first rows. This is the first and simplest way of creating oriental string work, which we are also going to be using around the top of the cake.

6 On the four equal-length sides of the cake, pipe bulbs along the top, making sure you pipe equal-sized bulbs and the same number of bulbs on each side. Make sure the rows of bulbs are right on the edges of your cake.

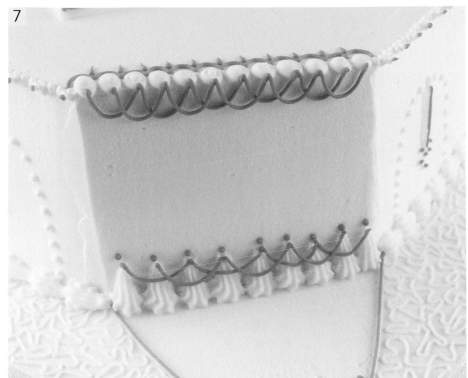

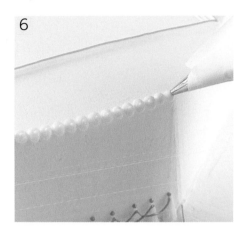

7 Using a no. 1 piping tube, pipe a loop which hangs from one bulb, misses one and attaches to the next bulb, just as you did to the shells around the base. Continue along the row and leave to dry. Now repeat the process, starting one bulb further over.

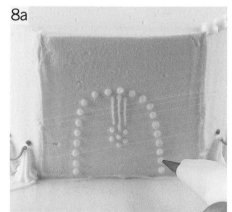

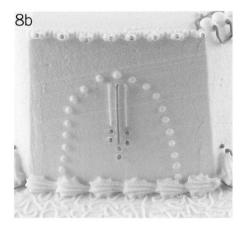

8 Make an archway-shaped template and scribe around it on each of the two small ends of the cake. Scribe two archways on each of the long sides of the cake. Pipe dots around all these arches. Then with a no. 1 tube pipe straight lines hanging down from the centre of the dotted arches. At the bottom of each line, pipe two tiny dots to complete this section of the design.

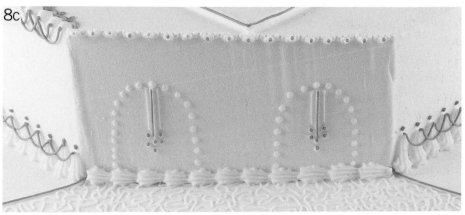

9 From the four short sides on which you have just piped your dotted-arch design, pipe a diagonal line with a no. 1.5 tube from the bottom edge of the cake out to the corner of the board. Do this for all four short sides.

10 Now pipe cornelli work with a no. 1 tube on the board between the lines you have just piped. Keep your cornelli neat and take your time. (See the section on cornelli work in piping techniques, page 60.)

11 On top of the cake, use a no. 1.5 tube to pipe a scalloped line to follow the line of the bulbs. Then overpipe this line with a no. 1 tube. This could be in a colour if you wish, or left white. Between each scallop you can pipe a single snail's trail.

12 Now pipe a small lace design along the top edge of each of the sides with the dotted-arch design. On the edge of the cake pipe tiny dots so that they touch all along the side. Then pipe a second row of dots, only this time pipe two dots, miss a dot, pipe two dots and so on, all the way along. On the third row pipe one dot in between every two and last of all pipe another single dot. This pattern looks great done in a colour to finish off the lace effect. Now repeat around the top on the other three dotted-archway sides.

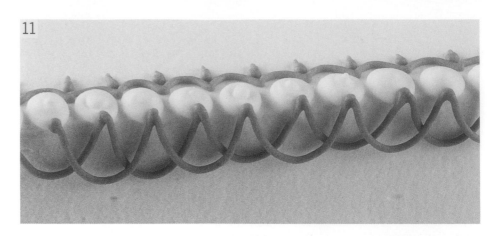

13 On the board you can pipe a line design on the four plain corners if you so wish. This cake looks good with colour added. Finish the cake with a ribbon around the board to match the colour you overpiped in. For the cake top to this cake, see page 114.

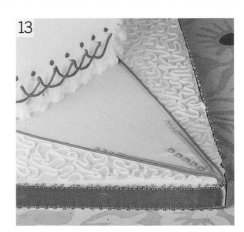

flooded monogram and butterfly cake

I have made this cake in a 25cm (10in) oval shape. I have then used two cake boards, one 7.5cm (3in) larger than the cake, and one 13cm (5in) larger than the cake. Whatever the size of your actual cake, use two boards 7.5cm (3in) and 13cm (5in) larger than the cake. I have glued the smaller board on top of the larger one. This cake is shown here in dramatic colours, but it would look extremely elegant all in one colour, with colour used only for the butterflies and ribbons. Never rush a cake such as this.

1 Royal-ice a round or an oval cake to a good finish and leave to dry. Do not ice the board at this stage. Using a side scraper with the cut-out design of your choice, give the sides a coat in the usual way by spreading on the icing using a palette knife (metal spatula). Then use your fancy side scraper to go around the sides of the cake. Leave to dry. There are many different side design scrapers you can choose from.

2 Attach the smaller board centred on top of the larger one using a glue stick. Leave it to dry. Now ice the boards in one of the methods from pages 56–7. I have used the flooding method. I did the top board first and just let the icing flow over the edge of the board so the side is coated. Then I went back and iced the base board.

3

3 Now you need to make a top collar template and a board template to fit the size of your cake. Try to make this up the day before you wish to use it. The collar is made in pastillage. Make a smaller board template to sit on the big one.

4 If you don't have a collar cutter, try cutting the pastillage with a pizza

4

wheel because it gives a good clean cut. Also cut out a selection of discs and hearts. Cut the pointed tips off the hearts so that you have a flat base to stick together – these will form the butterfly wings. Leave everything to dry on foam.

5 For the base collars make up a large paper piping (decorating) bag, making sure there is no hole at the end. Spoon the icing into your bag and no more than half fill it. Your icing needs to be the same consistency as the icing you flooded your board with. Cut a tiny hole in the end of the bag.

6 Fill in the collar, making sure your icing gets right into the corners and runs evenly to the edge. Have a damp clean paintbrush to hand just in case you need to help the icing flow. Place your collars under a table lamp: the faster they crust, the better. Leave these to dry for a day.

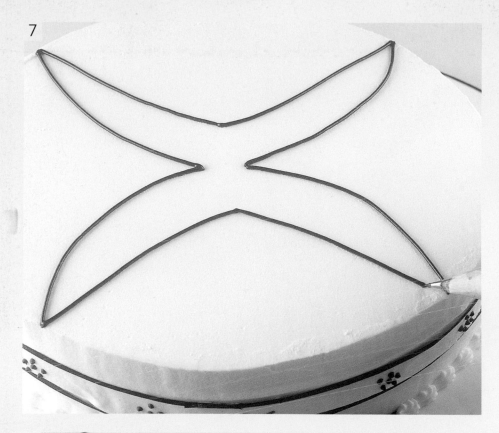

7

7 Take your cake-top template and scribe the top monogram design on your cake and outline with your no. 1 tube (nozzle).

8 When you fill this in you are working directly onto your cake, so do take your time to make sure you don't make any mistakes as it is much harder to correct. If you are unsure about flooding such an area directly onto a cake, flood it separately to the cake – as you did the collars. Then attach it to the cake with a line of piped icing once it is dry.

8

9 I have kept the design on the sides simple because we already have the collars. Between the lines on the side I have run round a double row of 3mm (⅛in) ribbon and joined the ribbons with a dot of icing, making sure that the join is at what will be the back of the cake. I have then piped a simple yet striking dot design in black. Place your cake on a turntable and glue a 15mm (⅝in) ribbon around the exposed edge of both the boards, joining the ribbons at the back of the cake. On the base board run a 3mm ribbon in the centre of the 15mm ribbon if you want a complementary colour.

10a

piece of foam underneath. Repeat this procedure for all the butterflies on the cake and the base boards.

12

10b

top of the cake. Pipe a design in black on the edge of the two collars – I have just continued with the simple dot design.

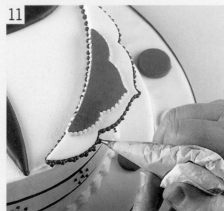

11

10 Pipe a snail's trail on the bottom of the collar, ready to stick on the cake. Place the collar in position, making sure it sits on the cake overlapping the edge by about 1cm (¹/₂in).

11 Once the collars are in position and are dry, attach the circles to sit wherever you choose to place them. Also place a circle in the centre of the

12 Dust the hearts with your chosen colour or moisten them with sugar glue and dip into your chosen glitter. Pipe bodies for the butterflies with a PME no. 4 piping tube and place the wings in position. You may need to support them in place with a

13 To finish you may decide to do the monograms. They can be piped and flooded with the run out icing directly onto the cake, or piped and flooded on to wax paper and then placed into position once dry.

13

14 The finishing touch is to go around the central oval with the same dot design and on the biggest board pipe a simple design. Around the top of the cake between both the collars I have used a no. 3 tube and piped a small scroll design.

monograms and run-out letters

Computers will enable you to experiment with different typefaces and sizes of letters, to create a variety of different templates. Also experiment with different arrangements of letters – in a straight line, or perhaps more quirky and jumbled up. But remember that some customers may have their own preference.

If you don't have access to a computer, don't worry. You can draw letters freehand using the templates provided for you in this book (see pages 157–8). I have given you two different fonts to choose from. You can photocopy the letters to the desired size.

You can write a complete name on the cake either by scribing directly onto the cake or by making the letters first on greaseproof (waxed) paper and positioning them on the cake when they are dry. This second way guarantees even spacing between the letters.

Outline your letters with a no. 1 tube (nozzle), then fill them in with the run-out icing. Make sure you keep the points on the letters sharp by guiding the icing in with a fine damp paintbrush.

using stencils

If you find you are struggling with some of the piping techniques, don't despair. Shop-bought or handmade stencils can be used with royal icing. Embroidery books are a great place to find sources for designs. Place the stencil in position on the cake. Spread a little royal icing across the stencil very thinly with your palette knife (metal spatula). Lift the stencil straight off and not at an angle, as you don't want to damage your work. You can use stencils on the sides of cakes as well as on the top. You can get a great effect by using them straight on the cake board as well.

4 sugar flowers

simple wired and unwired flowers

This chapter shows a selection of flowers that look as good wired as they do unwired. If you have never made a sugar flower before, unwired flowers are a good place to start.

The advantage of unwired flowers is they can be incorporated as part of the design of your cake without the worry of removing them before cutting the cake. You can purchase flower paste readymade from all sugarcraft shops. This guarantees that the consistency of the product is the same every time you use it, as it can be difficult to make two batches of home-made flower paste the same. Flower paste does, however, freeze beautifully and, if you make your own, it is worth freezing it in small lumps wrapped in cling film (plastic wrap), then in a small plastic bag. See page 156 for the recipe for flower paste.

To make flowers with flower paste you do need special equipment, but you will find you use the tools over and over again.

See pages 12–13 for details on the general equipment needed. Each project has its own list of specific requirements.

I have presented these flowers in order of the simplest first, but with patience and a little practice you will soon be able to master them all.

A small word of warning. You will find flower paste picks up dirt off your hands very easily and it can soon make the paste look grey. Also, if the atmosphere is dusty you will start finding bits appearing in your icing. All flower paste flowers which are dusted need steaming to show them off at their best. This cannot be done with unwired flowers as it can be dangerous (see right).

A simple rule to follow when arranging or wiring together flowers is to always work with an odd number never an even number. An odd number is always much more pleasing to the eye so keep this in mind when you make your flowers.

how to steam

Take a saucepan and two-thirds fill with water. Bring it to a rolling boil over the heat and only then turn the heat down. You will see lots of gentle steam. Pass the flowers or leaves gently and slowly through the steam, which is just enough to set the petal dust. Do not leave it so long it sends the paste soft and your flowers flop. If the steam slows down, just turn heat under the saucepan up again until the water comes to a rolling boil, then turn down again. It can be dangerous to use an electric kettle as the steam is so fierce. It is so easy to oversteam and turn the flowers soft, and until you have mastered steaming you can easily burn yourself in the steam of a kettle.

techniques

plunger blossoms

The plungers come in several sizes and the blossoms are very simple to make. They can also be made in either sugarpaste (rolled fondant or ready-to-roll icing) or flower paste.

You will need
- Plunger blossom cutter (selection of sizes) and rolling pin. To make as a centrepiece: 24g white wires and royal icing.

1 If you are using flower paste, lightly rub a tiny amount of white vegetable fat (vegetable shortening) into your board, then roll out the paste thinly. With your cutter, cut a flower and plunge it onto your balling mat so that it cups. This can then be left to dry or if you are brave you can plunge them directly onto your cake. Adhere by dabbing a dot of sugar glue where you wish to place the flower. Be careful; if you make a mistake it can mark your cake or you can easily squash the blossoms. I like to let them dry, then position the flowers on the cake with a dot of royal icing.

2 To finish the blossoms off, pipe a small coloured dot in the centre of each blossom. Make a piping bag, place green royal icing into the bag and cut a small upside down 'v' in the end of the bag. Squeeze out the icing to make little green leaves.

3 To make blossoms on stamens, take some small headed stamens. Cut some in half and on others just cut the head off one end, so you have two different lengths. Make a plunger blossom and whilst it is still wet, thread the stamen through the centre of the blossom. Secure in place with a dab of glue or pipe a coloured centre with royal icing. Tape the stamens together in clusters of three and five. Tape the cluster to a wire, keeping it neat and tidy. As I used silver wires I used white tape and painted the white tape with silver dust so that it all co-ordinates.

4 To put a larger plunger blossom on a wire, cut some of your wires in half and some into three, so you end up with different lengths of wire. Place a small hook on the end of the wire, then bend it so it lays flat. Push this wire through the blossom and pipe the centre in, continuing the colour theme. To dry the heads, place them in flower oasis with the head bent over. This way they will dry without the hook showing through the royal icing.

For a finished example of this cake, see the forget-me-not cake on page 37 and detail below.

petal blossom

These are simple unwired blossoms but the beauty of them is that they can be made in advance and put away until required. The blossoms come in several sizes and are very simple to make. They look great on a children's cake.

You will need

- Five-petal blossom cutters, rolling pin, balling tool and mat, flower paste, sugar glue, coloured semolina or gelatine, petal dust and brush.

1 Lightly rub into your board a tiny amount of white vegetable fat if required, then roll out the flower paste thinly. Cut out two five-petal blossoms per complete flower. These look good in coloured paste. Place the blossoms on your balling mat and ball the edges to give movement.

2 Place some glue in the centre of the first blossom, then place the other on top so that the top petals lie between the base petals. Press your bone tool in the middle of the blossom. Leave to set in a flower former, or if you don't have one use silver foil to make a little former, and place your flower in it.

3 Take a pea-sized piece of paste and flatten slightly, glue the top of the centre and throw into a pot of coloured semolina or gelatine. You colour the semolina by adding some petal dust to the semolina and mixing the two together. Place some glue on the centre, then place your centre in the middle of your flower. Finish off by dusting the edges of your blossom. To get a darker colour on the edge, brush from the outside in (see tip). To get a very dark colour on the edge, pull your flat brush across the edge of the petal from the front of the flower to the back.

tip

The dust should always be put on a piece of kitchen paper (paper towel) and the brush rubbed over the dust to break down the grains, so the dust is in the brush, not on the tip of the brush. This stops the grains flying about everywhere and dust getting where it's not wanted. Petal dusting adds an extra depth of colour to a flower and may be done in a very similar colour to the overall flower or in a complementary shade.

pulled filler flowers

For these flowers, the smaller-sized pea of paste you start with, the smaller the flower will end up being.

You will need

- 28g wire, flower paste, non-stick small stick, scissors or sharp knife, and petal dust.

1 Use 28g wire that has been cut into three pieces and bend a tiny hook on one end of each. Roll a pea of paste into a cone in the palm of your hand, making sure it is smooth and free from cracks. Then place the cone onto your non-stick small stick to open up the larger end.

2 Remove the cone from the stick and with a small pair of scissors make five cuts. Start by making a single cut, then equally place the other four cuts to produce five petals. Each cut should go down the cone by about two-thirds. Open up the petals a little

and round the edges of each petal by squeezing the tips.

3 Pinch the tips of each petal to round them further. Hold each petal between your thumb and first finger, and make a pinch-and-pull movement which flattens and widens each petal. These will not look as delicate as flowers made with a cutter, but you can get them reasonably fine.

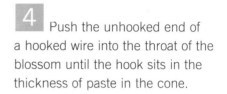

4 Push the unhooked end of a hooked wire into the throat of the blossom until the hook sits in the thickness of paste in the cone.

5 Dust up the flowers, with the method described on page 82, to finish. These make great filler flowers and can be adapted to fit in with any design you are using. You can try making four-petal blossoms instead of five, or you can put stamens in the centre of the flowers. Use a colour scheme that will complement the cake.

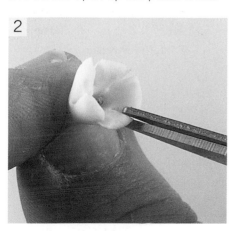

violets

You will need

- Flower paste, cell stick, scissors or sharp knife, 28g wire, sugar glue, petal dust and brush, and alcohol.

1 Make a small paste cone and open up the larger end on your cell stick. Cut the opened up end into five petals; two small, two medium and one larger petal. Pinch and pull each petal individually. Place the cone on a 28g wire. The wire should come out of the flower halfway down the hat on the underside of the cone.

2 The petals need to be arranged in a set position. The top two little petals lean back, the two sides petals come forwards and the large petal hangs down. Finish off by adding two tiny yellow paste ovaries at the front.

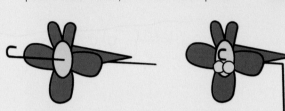

3 The flower is dusted with the main colour. Remember violets come in several colours and the centre is painted. Mix the yellow dust with a little alcohol. When that layer is dry, paint on fine black lines. These can be made wired or unwired.

arum lily

You will need

- Flower paste, rolling pin, arum lily cutter, plastic cocktail stick (toothpick), 26g wire, sugar glue, yellow semolina, veiner, balling mat and tool, and petal dust and brush.

entre – spadix

1 Knead a small amount of flower paste until it is smooth. Roll the paste into a very thin cigar shape.

2 Measure your centre against your arum lily cutter; it needs to be about two-thirds of the cutter's height. For the unwired version, place each centre onto a plastic cocktail stick greased with a small amount of white vegetable fat (shortening). For the

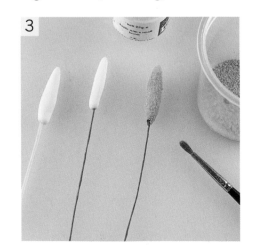

wired version, use a 26g wire cut into three to insert into a centre. Make sure the top of the piece of paste is rounded off slightly. Push the sticks into a piece of flower oasis covered in cling film (plastic wrap). Leave to dry.

3 Once the centres are dry, brush glue onto them and dip them in a mixture of semolina, or powdered gelatine mixed with food dusts, to get the colour you require. Leave to dry.

Petal – spathe

1 Lightly rub a tiny amount of white vegetable fat into your board, until you cannot see it. Knead a small knob of flower paste, then roll out the paste with your non-stick rolling pin. It helps to lift the paste and turn it around, but don't turn it over. You may find you need a palette knife (metal spatula) to help you lift the paste. Keep rolling until your paste is very thin. With white paste the trick to try is to see if you can read your newspaper through it; when you can, you are then ready to cut out.

2 If you have rolled enough paste to cut out more than one petal, keep the rest under a piece of cling film to prevent it drying out or place a small pot upside down over the top of it.

3 Place the petal on the balling mat and, using the thin end of your veining tool, mark veins so that they fan out from the base of the petal.

4 Next, take your ball tool and, with the tool half on the paste and half on the mat, apply a little pressure and go around the sides of the petal, stroking from the base to the point.

Do one side, then the other – you should notice it now has movement.

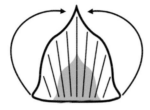

5 Place a little green dust onto a piece of kitchen paper (paper towel), then rub the grains of dust into your brush. This ensures that the dust is broken down and does not flick everywhere. Dust on a small amount of green to cover two-thirds of the petal from the base up.

6 Place a small amount of glue along the base of the petal and a maximum of a quarter of the way up the left side.

7 Take your completed centre and place it on the right of the petal, with the base of the centre in line

with the base of the petal. Roll the petal around the centre. Leave to dry.

8 To complete your flower, dust a small amount of green very faintly up the back of the flower. If the back isn't going to show when it is on the cake, you can omit this stage.

9 For the unwired version, when it is dry and you have completed dusting, hold the flower between your middle fingers and twist the cocktail stick to remove it safely, holding the flower in your hand. Place in a box for safety or position straight on the cake, using a small amount of royal icing.

unwired poinsettia

I am showing a simple quick unwired poinsettia as the wired one is more complicated. This gives an effective look for a Christmas cake and can be made in a variety of sizes.

You will need
- Large calyx cutter, flower paste, rolling pin, balling tool and mat, and sugar glue.

1 Mix your flower paste to the required colour (poinsettias come in red, white, cream and pink). Roll the paste out flat and cut out the first layer.

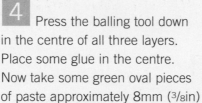

2 Place a central vein down each petal and ball the edges to give it some movement. Leave to one side of the balling mat. Now repeat the process with another two layers.

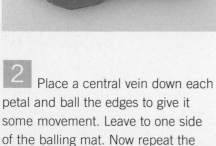

3 Place a dab of glue in the centre of the first layer and place the second layer on top of the first. Make sure the petals lay in between the petals of the first layer and do not overlap. Do the same with the third layer. These petals are called the "bracts".

4 Press the balling tool down in the centre of all three layers. Place some glue in the centre. Now take some green oval pieces of paste approximately 8mm (³/₈in) big and stick in the centre of the petals. If you wish, you can pipe these centres with royal icing instead.

5 To complete the poinsettia, pipe some yellow and red icing on top of the green paste or use small balls of yellow paste and snip into them to give the effect of little stamens.

daisy

You will need

- Flower paste, rolling pin and board, daisy cutter, 26g wire, balling tool and mat, former, sugar glue, petal dust and brush, cotton tulle net or sieve and yellow semolina.

1 Knead the paste ready for use and thinly roll it out. Cut out using the daisy cutter – you need two cut-out flowers per daisy.

2 For wired daisies cut a 26g wire into three. With each piece make a small hook at the top of the wire, then fold it flat.

3 Using your ball tool and working on your balling mat, ball each petal of the daisy from the outside tips in towards the centre so that the petals slightly curl, remembering to exert a little pressure as you do this. Place one set of petals on top of the other in a former, by placing a dab of glue between the two layers. Make sure

the petals of the second layer lay in between the petals of the first layer. With your balling tool on your mat, press down in the centre of your daisy.

4 For wired daisies, at this stage make a small hole in each daisy slightly off centre with a piece of wire so you can thread the hooked wire through later.

5 Once the petals are dry, brush a small amount of pale green in the centre. You do need to be able to see this just slightly once you have put the centres in.

6 To complete the unwired version, colour some flower paste yellow. Take a tiny ball of yellow flower paste and press it into a piece of cotton tulle net or into a sieve (strainer). This gives you a textured stamen surface. Brush a small amount of glue into the middle of the daisy and place the centre in position.

7 For the wired version, take a very small pea of paste and take one of your flat hooks. Dip the hook into the glue, then press the wire into the pea of paste. You then have a choice of two methods for the centre. You can use the net or sieve as in the unwired daisy or you can glue only

the top of the pea of paste and dip it into yellow semolina. To join the two pieces together, place some glue on the base of the centre and pull through the ready-made hole. Leave to dry.

8 To complete, take your smallest-sized daisy cutter and with green flower paste cut out one layer. Place a little glue on the underneath of the daisy, thread the calyx up the wire and position on the base of the daisy.

See page 66 for a simple daisy side design cake. If you are making a wired spray or arrangement you do need daisy leaves; see also the section at the end of the of this chapter (page 100) where I look at simple foliage.

small filler orchid

You will need

- 28g wire, flower paste, non-stick pin, rolling pin and board, single petal cutter, balling tool and mat, sugar glue, small calyx cutter, non-stick small stick, veining tool and petal cutter.

1 These are best made on a 28g wire cut into three pieces. You do not require a hook. Roll a tiny cone of white paste and insert your wire.

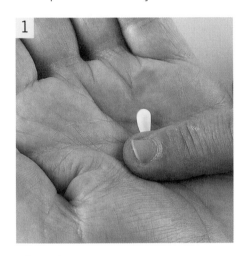

2 In your fingers, roll the base of the cone to elongate it so it is two-thirds the height of the petal cutter you are using. Press the end of a paintbrush or non-stick pin in the side of the cone to cup it. It should look like a tiny spoon. Leave to dry.

3 Roll out a piece of flower paste and cut out a petal for the tongue. If you use a five petal cutter you can then cut them into individual petals

and keep the rest under plastic to stop them drying out. Place your petal on your balling mat and ball around the edge with a bone/balling tool.

4 Stick this around the base of the shaped cone with a tiny amount of glue. Leave to dry for a short time.

5 Now make a cone, double the size you made for the centre. With your fingers start pulling the paste out from the large end of the cone until you have something that resembles a pointy hat. Now with your small non-stick pin roll the paste from the rim of the 'hat' on your board working from the centre out to get your paste thin. You may need to make the centre cone slightly thinner, do this by rolling it between your thumb and first finger. When the paste is thin enough then place your cutter over the centre and cut out your calyx. This is called the Mexican hat method.

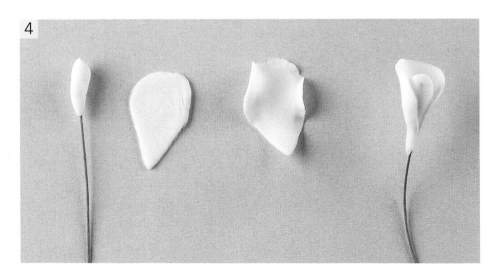

6 Now hold the calyx between your thumb and first finger, and open up the throat slightly by inserting your non-stick small stick into the centre. Now with your veining tool put one central vein down each petal.

7 Next on your balling mat ball each petal from the outside to the centre. Now glue lightly in the throat you have made and insert your wire with the spoon and tongue on. Position it so it just sits in the hole in the throat where you have glued. You may feel you need to thin the back down, but just roll it again between your thumbs and first finger, and pinch off any excess to reuse.

This is an ideal flower to use as filler flower in a spray or simply as a wired stem of dainty baby orchids on a cake.

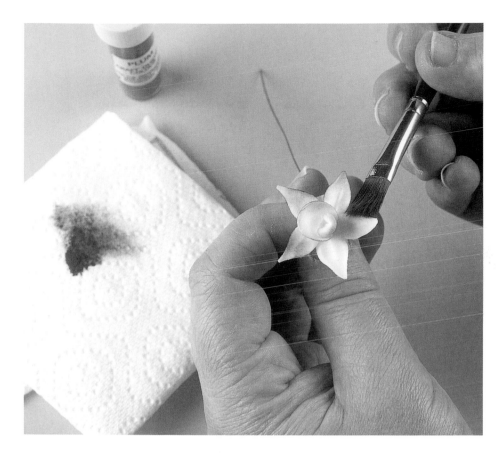

Unwired flower

I do not use this as an unwired flower very often as the spoon-shaped centre always has to be that little more bulky but if you wish then just make the spoon on a greased plastic cocktail stick (toothpick) and proceed as above. They do look very effective on little cup cakes as they are so dainty.

Dusting of the flower

You have only to look in a flower book or on the Internet to see how many different colours the flowers come in. Dust in colours to suit your requirements, but make sure you use

the dust from a piece of kitchen paper (paper towel), not straight from the pot (see above). Rub the colour into your brush to break the granules down to get a much better finish. If you want your orchids to have dots, use a very fine sable paintbrush (0 or 00) and dust mixed with a spot of alcohol. Never use the paste colours neat as they will not dry properly.

orchid

You will need

- Flower paste, 24g white wire, non-stick small stick, veining tool, knife, sugar glue, rolling pin and board, balling tool and mat, orchid cutter set, petal dust and brush.

Spoons

1 There are numerous different colour schemes that can be used for orchids, so the spoons, tongues and petals may all need to be coloured or made in a variety of coloured pastes. Take a pea-sized ball of paste and roll into a cone with quite a long tail. Using a 24g white wire, wire the cone from the pointed end, ensuring the wire is fed up one side of the cone.

2 On the opposite side from the wire, press into the cone with a non-stick small stick to produce the shape of a little spoon. Try to keep the back side rounded and the edges quite thin. On the back side of the spoon shape, use a veining tool to add a central line, two definite lines either side and fainter lines outside that.

3 Take a very small piece of yellow flower paste and roll into a sausage shape, about 1cm (1/2in). Make an indent in the centre with a knife, but do not cut all the way through. Add sugar glue to the inside tip of the spoon and glue these "ovaries" into place. Let the spoon dry

for at least 24 hours before proceeding with the next steps.

Tongues

1 Roll out a small amount of paste, but do not roll it as thin as for ordinary petals (as orchids are tropical and therefore have a slightly thicker feel to them). Cut out the tongue shape with the orchid cutter. Use the veining tool to add quite a few veins down the tongue. Ball the edges to heavily frill them.

2 Take a very small piece of yellow flower paste and roll into a sausage shape 2cm (3/4in) long. Flatten with a palette knife (metal spatula) and indent along the length to make it look like it is cut in half. Glue the yellow piece of paste to the tongue from the base upwards. It should come about three-quarters of the way up the tongue. Add sugar glue to the base of the spoon and bend the head back with the curved side outermost.

3 Lay the spoon down onto the tongue and wrap the tongue around

the spoon. Squeeze into place and dry upside down. The spoon should be sitting slightly away from the tongue, but can be dried in a variety of positions, to give different stages of orchid development.

Petals

4 Roll out a small amount of paste, making a centre vein with the central vein rolling pin, but do not roll it as thin as for ordinary petals. Cut out the petal shape with the orchid cutter. For cymbidium and cattleya orchids, three of the longer petals and two of the shorter petals are required, although all petals can be made of the same shape depending on the overall effect required.

5 Insert the wire about a quarter of the way into the petal only. Wires

5

are always inserted into the rounder end of the petal.

6 Add veins up the length of the petal with a veining tool. Ball the edges, always working from the wire to the end of the petal, to keep the shape of the petal even.

7 Petals may be dusted at this stage, or may be dusted once the full orchid has been constructed.

9a

Construction

8 Bend all the petals back on their wires until they are nearly at a 90-degree angle.

9 Add the two "arms" to the tongue. They should go either side of the tongue. Add the "head". This is the petal that goes opposite to the tongue. Add the two "legs". For an orchid, the tongue always hangs down between the legs.

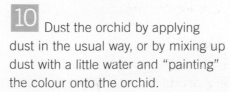

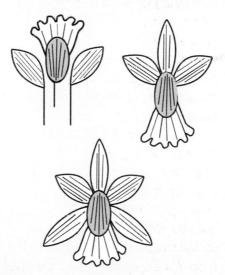

9b

10 Dust the orchid by applying dust in the usual way, or by mixing up dust with a little water and "painting" the colour onto the orchid.

sweet peas

You will need

- 26g wire, white and green flower paste, sugar glue, rolling pin and board, sweetpea cutters, balling tool and mat, calyx cutter, cocktail stick (toothpick).

Wired

1 Cut a 26g wire into three and make a small hook on the end, then fold the hook over again to make a little D on the top of the wire.

2 Using your chosen colour flower paste, take a small pea of paste and roll it into a ball. Place a dab of glue on the D hook and, from the flat back of the hook, press the pea of paste so it goes around the hook. Now with your fingers press the

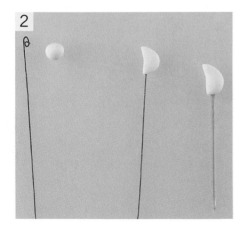

two sides of the paste around the D hook and pinch the edges together to a fine edge making it look like a small pod which contains a pea,

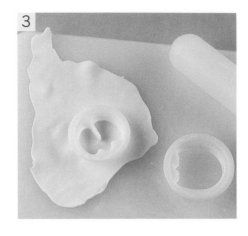

keeping the D shape. At the top of the pea, pinch the paste back to a small point. Leave this to dry.

3 Now finely roll out your paste. Cut out the paste with the flower cutter that looks like two wings (sweetpea cutter).

4 Place your cut-out piece onto your balling mat and ball with your bone tool all around the edge, applying pressure to really frill the wings. Place a little glue down

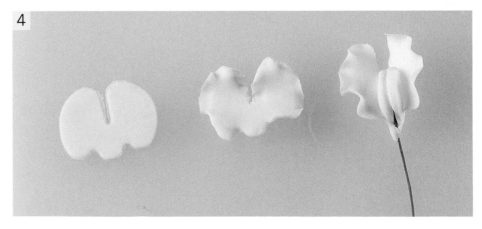

the centre of the wings and sit the wings on the pea so that the little point on the pea goes back between the wings and the little U piece at the base of the wings sits around the wire at the base of the pea.

5 Place your wings to dry so that the wings come forwards slightly by bending the head of the wire. Now roll out your paste and cut your back piece using the large cutter in the set. Place on your balling mat and frill with your balling tool to give lots of movement. Glue down the centre, but only the bottom two-thirds. Place behind the wings again, placing the U in the same place as you did for the wings. This piece can be left in whatever position it sits best as you will find that, with sweet peas, the older the flower, the further back this piece leans. So, if it is just opening from the bud stage it will be leaning forwards. Leave to dry.

6

6 Now take green flower paste and roll out a piece slightly thicker than the petals and cut out a small five pointed calyx. Just soften the edges on your balling mat and place a dab of glue in the centre and on two of the petals. Stick your wire through the centre of the calyx so that the two glued petals stick up the back of the flower and the other three turn down at the front of the flower.

Unwired

7 Take a pea of paste and in your fingers mould the pea in a pod shape as described above for the wired sweet peas. Place on a lightly greased plastic cocktail stick. Proceed to make the rest of the sweet pea as in the wired section. You will find you will need to position the wings as you cannot bend the head to dry.

8 You need to remove the sweet pea from the stick before you put the calyx on. This can be done by placing the flower head between your fingers and twisting the stick, so that when the head comes off you have it safe in your hand.

9 Now follow the procedure for the wired calyx to place a calyx on each sweet pea.

Finishing touches

Sweet peas come in such a variety of colours from pastel to deep colours. A lot are white with a coloured edge. Dust up carefully and don't add too much dust in one go. Remember you can always go over it again to make the colour deeper but it's a lot more difficult to remove the colour. To complete your sweet peas make a few tendrils by taking half a 30g green wire and wrapping it around your non-stick pin or a paint brush. Remove from the stick and wire into the spray or if you are piping the stems on a cake and using the unwired heads, just pipe the tendrils by piping a circular movement to give the effect you require.

rose

You will need

- Coloured and white flower paste, 24g or 26g wire, rolling pin and board, five-petal blossom cutter, balling tool and mat, paintbrush, calyx cutter.

Buds

1 Start by making your cones on 24g or 26g wires that have been cut into three. Hook the end of each. Your cones should be about two-thirds of the size of a petal on your cutter.

2 Next take your coloured paste, roll out very finely and cut a set of petals. Slightly ball the head and two legs on your balling mat with your balling tool. Leave the arms.

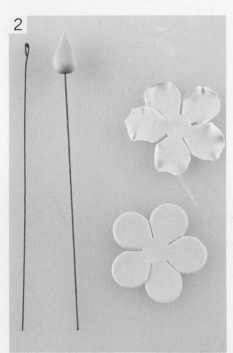

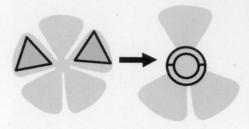

3 Turn the flower over and then, taking a cone, insert the wire through the centre of the petals and hold between your fingers so the petals lay flat in your hand. Glue one of the arms and cuddle it around the cone very tightly; repeat with the second arm.

4 Now with a fine brush place a little glue on the bottom two-thirds of all three petals, on one edge only; however, it must be on the same edge on all three petals. Now position all three petals on to the cone, then glue the bottom two-thirds on the other edge of the petals and stick down. Your petals should be overlapping each other. This is the stage you decide how tight you want your bud or how much to curl it back. The tighter you put them around the cone, the tighter the bud will be, or you can curl the petals back slightly as if the bud is just opening.

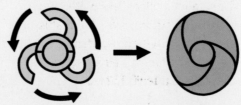

Half rose

5 Take your paste and add about a quarter of white paste. Mix together to get a paler shade than you have used so far; this is because the outside petals on a rose are lighter than the inside ones. Roll out your paste and cut a second layer; this time ball and frill all the petals to give lots of movement, then turn over. You can curl some of the petal edges back with a cocktail stick (toothpick) at this stage if you wish. Place on the wire as before and hold between your fingers in your hand. Glue two-thirds of the edge of one side of the petals as you did for the bud and place around the bud. Then glue in the same way on the other side of the petal. This creates a half rose. Play about with the petals until you get them how you want – petals curling back or still quite tight.

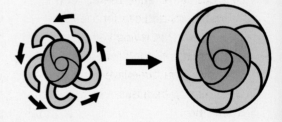

Full rose

6 Make your paste paler again by a quarter of white paste. Then follow the instructions for the half rose. Try to start laying your petals in the middle of the previous petals. This gives you three layers in all. Leave to dry, then dust up if required when dry.

Calyx

7 To make the calyx make a Mexican hat in green and roll the paste out with thin edges. Cut out your calyx and ball to soften the edges. As roses vary according to their variety, cut into the calyx, or leave the cuts out. Open up the throat, place a little glue in the throat and place calyx on back of rose. The Mexican hat is then pushed up to make a hip. Alternatively, roll out your green paste flat, cut out a calyx and soften. Put in cuts as shown right, put the rose through the centre and glue in place. Then mould the shape of a hip, dab a little glue on the back of the calyx and push it up the wire into place. This is the easier method; however, the first is more natural. When dry, dust up the hip with brown, red and green dust to give a realistic finish.

See page 100 for rose leaves.

carnation

You will need

- 26g wire, florist tape, flower paste, rolling pin and board, carnation cutter, veining tool, sugar glue, small calyx cutter, scissors, petal dust and brush.

1 Cut a 26g wire into three and make a small hook on each end. Using white tape, tape over the hook. Keep it very small and neat. Colour up your paste and roll it out thinly, cut out using your cutter, this time leaving your carnation layer on your rolling-out board. If you cut more than one, do remember to cover the paste with plastic to prevent them drying out.

2 Now using your veining tool press on the layer, working on one scallop at a time to thin it; this veins it as well. You will see that when the layer starts to thin it will spread and frill.

3 When you have gone all the way around thinning and frilling, place some glue in the middle and insert your wire through the centre of the layer. Take it up to the hook and fold the layer in half over the hook.

4 Now you need to fold both the side pieces in, so place a dab of glue at the base of the flower on the left side and fold into the centre, making sure the head all remains at the same height. Now turn your flower round and repeat with the other side. The turning in of the sides has been done to produce a letter Z, if this helps you to remember. Squeeze the base to keep it thin and remove any

1

where you squeezed the base of the layers. Roll between your fingers to thin the Mexican hat if you need to. Don't make the Mexican hat too long because the calyx on a carnation is quite bulbous.

excess paste if you feel it is needed. This makes the bud or you can continue to the full flower. Leave this stage to dry so the following two stages are put onto a dry base.

5 Layers two and three are identical. Repeat the frilling that you did for the first layer, glue the central half of the layer, insert the wire with your dry layer on and take the layer

up the wire. It helps if you hold the wire between your fingers so you are supporting the layer in your hand. Take the second layer up and squeeze around the dry first layer making sure the top of the head of the carnation is level and has not dropped down. Now repeat once again for a full-blown carnation.

6 Take some green paste and a small five-pointed calyx cutter. Using the Mexican hat method as described for the small filler orchid (see page 88), cut out a calyx. Thin each point with your balling tool, but try not to stretch them, then open up the throat.

7 Glue in the centre of the throat and push the flower wire through the centre of the throat. Push the calyx right up to the carnation so it sits over

8 To finish off, turn the flower upside down and snip two little cuts opposite each other, then just below those. Do another four, but on the opposite sides to the two you have just done. Now to dust up the carnation, just rub the flat side of the brush across the top of the flower. Quite often on carnations the tips are a deeper colour or a contrasting colour.

chocolate lilies

You will need
- Flower paste, rolling pin and board, former, lily cutters, paintbrush, chocolate moulding icing or royal icing, and veining tool.

Stamens

Roll pieces of paste out thinly between your fingers about 5cm (2in) maximum in length. Create a point at one end as if the pollen has been removed or make a little T bar on it if you want to give the effect of the pollen still attached. Make six of these per lily and squeeze them together at the base of the stamens. Leave to dry ready for the flower.

Petals

1 Set your former out on a clean surface, thin end facing up. Roll out your paste as thin as you can get it on a light dusting of icing (confectioners') sugar and cut the three smaller petals in the set. Vein the petals with the veiner from the set and place all three around the former. Squeeze the petals

together at the top. The petals will curl back on the board slightly, pinch off any excess paste to reuse. At every stage dust off any icing sugar that is on your petals.

2 Now roll out the paste to cut out the larger three petals. Place these so that they lay in between the bottom three petals and again join at the top.

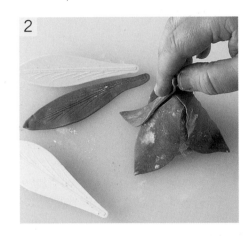

3 The petals should all stick together well, but if you have problems just use a damp paintbrush to go over the paste – this will make it stick. Pinch off the excess paste at the top and leave the flower to dry overnight. If you want to carry on making more, just make yourself a cardboard cone to use for the lily former.

4 When the flowers are dry, remove from the former and stick the stamens in the middle with either a

small fresh ball of chocolate moulding icing (see page 156 for recipe) or a dab of royal icing, making sure the colour matches.

Leaves

If I decide I need leaves for the lily I simply use the smaller of the two cutters, but to vein it I use my veining tool. Only the central vein on a leaf is straight; the others radiate from the stem base and gradually curve out and all come back up to meet at the tip. Bend the leaves so they have some movement.

Chocolate arum lilies

These can also be made in chocolate. Follow the instructions for unwired arum lilies (see page 85). You make the spadix one colour and the spathe another, which looks stunning. A touch of gold dusting always looks good on chocolate.

chocolate roses

You will need

- Flower aste, plastic bag, knife, petal dust and brush. For leaves: rose leaf plunger cutter and veiner or rose leaves, chocolate and paintbrush.

1 Start by making a cone with a neck and a small base.

2 Now make some balls half the size of the piece of paste you started with. Make them all equal size and cone them slightly, these are for your petals. Place them in a small plastic bag to keep them soft.

3 Working on one cone at a time, place it into another plastic bag and press to flatten the cone. Make it as thin as possible.

4 Remove from the bag and just finger the petal around the edges and place it around the cone made in step 1. Continue placing each petal on one at a time, gradually curling the petals out for a full-blown rose. When you are happy with your flower just cut the rose off at the neck and leave it to dry.

5 There is no right or wrong numbers of petals to use, and you

4b

usually need a variety of sizes for a good realistic finish. For that special touch, when they are dry dust the edges with gold dust, which really does give a rich finish to your roses. White roses can be dusted on the edges with a colour if you wish.

Leaves

Method one

Roll out the modelling paste and, with a rose leaf plunger cutter, cut and vein the leaves. Twist and shape to give movement.

Method two

Take some real rose leaves from the garden, wash them and dry them thoroughly. Melt some chocolate and brush it on the back of the rose leaf. Leave to set. Then peel the leaf back to reveal the chocolate rose leaf.

Although method two is fiddly, the leaves you produce look extremely effective. Method one is quicker, however, and the leaves work well.

4a

foliage

You will need

- 28g wire, coloured flower paste, rolling pin and board, veiner, leaf cutters, petal dust and brush, balling tool, confectioners' glaze with IPA, florist tape and tweezers.

Rose leaves

1 Have a 28g green wire ready, cut into three. Roll the flower paste into a sausage, then with your rolling pin roll out to flatten the paste. Using a centre-veining pin, roll over the paste to create a wire groove or use a grooved rolling board.

2 Cut out the leaves with a rose leaf cutter. You need two different sizes, for each set of leaves you need one large leaf and four smaller leaves, with the largest leaf

at the top. Push the 28g wire up into the centre vein.

3 Vein with the rose leaf veiner or mark the veins with the veining tool and ball the edges to give the leaf movement. When dry dust up with moss green and foliage green. On the edges of the leaves use brown and red, depending on what effect you hope to achieve.

4 To wire the leaves together, take your large leaf and two of your smaller leaves. Place the two smaller leaves just beneath the large leaf and tape them in opposite each other, then place two more smaller ones beneath those and tape into place. There should be just a small stem showing on each leaf. Steam the leaves at this stage (see page 80).

Violet leaves

Roll out green paste with a centre vein, cut out various-sized heart-shaped leaves, insert a 28g wire and vein either with a violet leaf veiner or an ivy veiner. Ball slightly round the edges but do not frill as they are quite a flat leaf. They need a much darker dusting on the top than underneath.

Daisy leaf

This is a fiddlier leaf to produce and it always seems so fragile. To make it use exactly the same method as for the rose leaf, but use the multi-purpose veiner. When dry, just lightly dust the surface of the leaf and not

Daisy leaf

Ivy leaf

the underneath. Handle carefully – this leaf is so thin in places that this is the time it is likely to break.

Ivy

Roll out the flower paste thinly with a centre vein up the middle and cut out several different sizes of leaves. Cut a 28g wire into four and insert the wire into the vein about halfway up. Vein the leaves with a veiner, then soften the edges with a balling tool to give movement.

Green ivy

Make all your ivy leaves in a green flower paste and once the leaves are dry dust over them with a green dust that suits the shade you require. If you look at green ivy it really does vary in shades. Steam all the ivy and if you want a shiny finish to your ivy you can just brush over it with a glaze. Use confectioners' glaze mixed with IPA to thin it down or just buy a light glaze which you brush on as it is.

Variegated ivy

Make the base of the ivy in a cream paste. The cream base does vary on real plants, but if you don't want it to look yellow keep it a very pale cream. Leave the leaves to dry. Now take your green dust and dust your green onto the leaf going from the base of the leaf up, remembering to leave a gap of cream all the way

around the edge. The back also needs doing, but it is always lighter than the front of the leaf. Steam the leaves to set the dust.

Another method if you want a darker green is to paint the green dust on. Mix the dust with a little alcohol or water, and using a sable brush paint the green onto the leaf. They give different effects so only you can decide which you like best.

To assemble ivy

Remember, to achieve the best results, start with the smaller leaves, leaving approximately 2.5cm (1in) of stem on each leaf and tape onto the main stem so that the leaves overlap just by the tip of their point.

Keep taping leaves in until you have the correct amount, then, holding the wire of the first leaf and the stem at the base, bend the stem to give a more natural finish. Now with your tweezers, lift each leaf and bend the leaf over at the top and spread them to the left and the right.

Assembling ivy

fillers and sprays

You will find all three of these fillers useful in flower sprays. In the cake top chapter, the use of curled wires is also described, but these really are only a decoration and not a filler. The other filler some people like to use, and this very modern, is feathers. People have mixed views on these, but I do feel they have a place in cake decorating. Do buy them from a specialist shop; this ensures that they are safe to use and germ-free. Feathers should not come directly into contact with the icing.

Making ribbon loops

Ribbon loops are useful as filler material; they also prevent flower heads knocking together and damaging each other, so act as a cushion. They are good to use in arrangements, 3mm (⅛in) ribbon is the best to use as it delicate and is not overpowering for most displays. Using ribbon loops is an excellent way of bringing colour to your flower sprays.

Triple loop with tails

Equipment
- Length of 30g wire, tape, 3mm (⅛in) ribbon

Method

1 Use your hand to loop the ribbon. With your palm facing you, rest the ribbon over the top of the index finger and pinch it between your ring and little finger.

2 Wrap the ribbon round your fingers three times. Pass the wire underneath the ribbon loops.

3 Twist the wire together to secure. Have one end of wire slightly longer than the other.

4 Remove the ribbon from your hand and pinch the base together. Wrap the shorter wire end around the base of the ribbon to keep the ribbon loops together.

5 Tape florist tape around the wire and base of ribbon loop to secure, and tape down the length of the wire. Cut the tails to your preferred length.

Glycerine gypsophila filler

This can be purchased from sugar-craft shops or florists. Do, however, make sure you are purchasing glycerine gypsophila and not dried; they are different. Dried would just fall apart in the spray.

Method

1 Pull the stem of glycerine gypsophila apart into small florets.

2 Place small clumps together and bind around the stems with a 30g wire that has been cut into three.

3 Tape from just above the bare wire right to the bottom of the stem with half-width florist tape.

Bear grass

This adds greenery to a floral display and gives a modern look. It acts as a cushion so adds extra protection to the flowers. It can be purchased from sugarcraft shops or a florist shop.

To add to displays, the bear grass can be wired and taped together into the legs of a wired flower spray. Bear grass can be used like ribbon to create loops, or may be left long to add height and interest to a display. The bear grass gets thicker towards the base of the stem; to save wasting this material if only the top part is used in a display, the plastic may be carefully cut into a point and used as additional stems in an arrangement.

Hogarth spray of roses and carnations

Equipment

- 1 standard full rose (3 layers)
- 6 standard half roses (2 layers)
- 3 standard rose buds (1 layer)
- 4 leaf units
- 2 carnation buds (1 layer)
- 2 medium carnations (2 layers)
- 2 large carnations (3 layers)
- 6 wired ribbon loops
- 6 wired gypsophila sprigs
- Half-width green tape

There is no defined way of putting together the spray. Different amounts of flowers and foliage may be used and they may be assembled in any position. This is just a suggestion for one possible presentation.

Before you start wiring have all your flowers laid out so you can see what you have. I always have everything to hand – wire cutters, tape etc. I lay my flowers on my rolling-out board and place the edge of a tea (dish) towel underneath the board so the other end sits on my lap. By doing this, if I drop a flower it does not drop on the floor but has a soft landing. As you make a leg, put identical flowers aside for the other leg so you know just what you have left for the central posy. If you do not wish to use gypsophila or ribbon loops, you will need to add a filler flower into the spray.

Method

1. For this spray, start with a stem of three rose leaves. To this, then tape in a rose bud to the left and a piece of gypsophila to the right.

2. Then place a piece of gypsophila and a ribbon loop to the left and a carnation bud to the right.

3. At this stage place a half rose to the left and a ribbon loop to the right followed by another half rose.

4. To complete this leg add a spray of five rose leaves on the left hand side.

5. Now repeat the process again to make a second identical leg, making sure you keep the same spacing between the flowers. Place both legs safely to one side.

6. Take your central full-blown rose and tape two ribbon loops opposite each other and two pieces of gypsophila on the opposite sides.

7. Now add the two medium carnations and two full-blown carnations. Sit them around the central rose.

8. Finally tape in the remaining two half roses and one rose bud.

9. You are now ready to start joining the two legs and central posy together; this is the hardest part of the whole procedure. Have small lengths of tape already cut off so you are not trying to sort out your tape while holding your flowers; do not try to work with the tape attached to the roll as this makes it very difficult to work.

10. Take your two identical legs and use your angled tweezers to help you bend the stem of each leg about 5cm (2in) from your last flower.

11. Take one leg at a time and the central posy – you will find the flowers naturally sit into each other. Keep both the posy and leg at the same height (it is so easy to drop the leg slightly). Now take your other leg and repeat the process, making sure the two legs are opposite each other.

12. The final stage is to bend your legs so they curve to form a letter S. This makes your Hogarth spray.

Teardrop arrangement

This is made from a posy just like you made for the Hogarth spray and one leg. The leg should be fuller and should end looking symmetrical or balanced.

Crescent arrangement

This is made from a central posy and two legs mirror imaged (as opposed to identical end sprays as for the Hogarth spray). It is assembled in an identical manner to the Hogarth spray.

(5) cake tops

All the cake tops use a variety of different mediums and I have stated which you should use for each project. Use these cake tops designs as a guide only; you can alter the colours and finishing touches to fit in with your style and design of cake.

mediums

Flower paste

This is a medium that is traditionally used to create sugar flowers. Flower paste dries to a strong finish, making it suitable for most cake tops. (See page 156 for the flower paste recipe.)

Sugarpaste

You can use the same paste that you coat your cake in to model lovely cake tops. Sugarpaste (rolled fondant or ready-to-roll icing) has a long drying time, giving you longer to model than the flower paste. (See page 154 for sugarpaste recipe.)

Pastillage

Pastillage is a very hard, fast-drying medium. It starts crazing within minutes. The recipe I have given for gelatine-based pastillage gives you slightly longer to work with (see page 156 for recipe). I have made two pastillage cake tops: one very simple one for a christening cake (see page 110); the other also includes a little simple modelling (see page 119).

Mexican paste

This has the beauty of giving you longer to work with. It still dries hard but it takes much longer to dry. Choose this paste if you need time to get the modelling correct.

cake top designs

daisy arrangement – flower paste

You will need

- Dry hard flower paste plaque in the shape of your choice, some excess sugarpaste (rolled fondant or ready-to-roll icing) in white to arrange the flowers in, a selection of 5–7 wired daisies and a few daisy leaves.

1 To finish this cake off, I made a little arrangement on a flower paste plaque. Prepare a selection of daisies and leaves. Knead ¼ teaspoon Tylo powder into 115g (4oz) flower paste and roll out. Cut your plaque to the required shape and size. Leave to dry on a piece of flat foam for 48 hours.

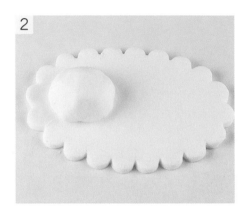

equal quantities of sugarpaste and flower paste mixed for the centre. The drying time will be quicker, so you will find you can start arranging in it sooner.

3 Start arranging your daisies in the centre of the plaque and work out. You can position your daisies individually or you can tape the daisies together in little bunches. Cut the wires down if necessary and push into the lump of paste using your angled tweezers. To finish off the arrangement, add some daisy leaves.

4 To complete your cake, place the arrangement in position. This can be removed from the cake and the arrangement kept to be used again.

2 Put a dab of sugar glue or squeeze some royal icing in the centre of the plaque and place a small blob of the sugarpaste with Tylo in the centre. Leave this for about 4 hours. Alternatively, you can use

christening cradle – pastillage

You will need

- Board, small rolling pin, pastillage, five-petal blossom cutters, non-stick pin, toy baby, no. 1 piping tube (nozzle), petal dust and brush, and plunger blossoms on stamens.

1 On a board that has been greased, roll out the pastillage thinly. Using a large-size blossom cutter cut two pieces and place them on a piece of foam to dry. If you want to be a little more adventurous, you can use the end of a no. 4 piping tube and make a small pattern in each petal of the blossom. Cut a plaque for the cradle to stand on and a base 5 x 4.5cm (2 x 1½in). Lay this over your rolling pin so the longer side runs along the length and so that it dries with a curve.

2 Put some white royal icing in a bag with a no. 1 tube. When all the pieces are dry, take one of the blossoms and the curved base and join together so that the curved base is in the middle of the blossom. The blossom piece is lying down flat with the curved base standing up. Pipe a small snail's trail inside the curved base to attach it on to the blossom. Leave to dry for at least 30 minutes.

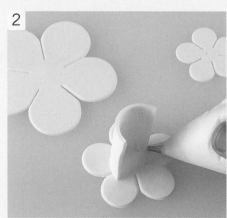

3 Now take the other blossom and turn the joined piece over. Line up the blossoms so they are at the same angle and the base is sitting in the same position and again pipe a snail's trail on the inside of the cradle. Leave to dry out thoroughly overnight.

4 Place the empty cradle in the centre of the plaque and attach it with a small dot of royal icing on the inside where it cannot be seen. Again, leave to dry.

5 Now you need to dress the cradle. You may find you need to fill the cradle out with a little sausage of sugarpaste (rolled fondant or ready-to-roll icing). Make a pillow by rolling out a piece of sugarpaste 0.5cm (¼in) thick, then cut a square out, 4.5cm (1½in) maximum. With your small non-stick pin, press in all around the edge of the pillow to frill. Squeeze a small amount of royal icing and position the pillow.

6 Place a plastic baby in the cradle. Make a blanket by rolling

out sugarpaste thinly and cutting out using a blossom cutter. Frill the edge of the sugarpaste and, with a no. 1 piping tube, pipe a pattern across the blanket. Hold the blanket in position with a squeeze of royal icing.

7 To finish, dust the edges of the pillow and blanket. I have finished my cradle off with a few of the plunger blossoms on stamens. I taped the clusters on to wires and,

with small bulbs of royal icing, attached the clusters behind the cradle head.

baby's bib — sugarpaste or flower paste

You will need
- Sugarpaste (rolled fondant or ready-to-roll icing) or flower paste, rolling pin and board, garret frill cutter, cel stick, a no. 2 or 3 piping tube (nozzle), petal dusting and brush, and 3mm (⅛in) ribbon or royal icing.

1 Start by rolling the sugarpaste or flower paste extra thinly and cutting one whole frill. Then, take the small centre of your cutter and cut out a section of the frill for the neck of the bib.

2 Frill around the bib as for the garret frill (see page 42). Take a no. 2 or 3 piping tube and use it as a cutter or embosser. Mark an embroidery pattern just above the frill. Leave it to dry, then use a dusting brush and petal dusts to dust over the edge of the frill.

3 To complete the design, add two ribbon ties on the neck. This can be done in 3mm ribbon or with narrow paste ribbons, or by piping them in with royal icing.

engagement or wedding cake top – mexican paste or pastillage

2 Take both the large frill circle and the large centre circle, and stick together with a dab of royal icing. Next, stick the medium circle on to base in the same way and leave to dry; now the base is ready for the next stage. If you wish to dust the edges of the base and the horseshoe, this is the stage to do it. Do be careful not to overdo the dusting; just remember you can add more easily than you can remove.

You will need

- Mexican paste or pastillage, garret frill cutter and centre cutters, heart cutter royal icing, petal dust and dusting brush.

- One large circle using the largest of the three centre circles.
- One smaller circle using the medium centre circle.
- Two hearts cut to about 4cm (1½in).

1 Roll out the paste to the same thickness as you would for a garret frill (see page 42). Cut out the following pieces and leave to dry overnight (see photos above for guidance):

- One frill circle using the largest centre. Cut out a section of the frill to make a horseshoe shape. If you so wish, at this stage you can use a no 1.52 tube (nozzle) to pattern the paste.
- One solid frill circle with centre still in place.

3 Use a royal icing bag with a small shell tube to pipe some royal icing in the centre of the circle. This will not be seen when completed so don't worry if it doesn't look perfect. Place the horseshoe into the icing

and, if necessary, pipe a little more icing either side of it to support it.

4 Lean the horseshoe against a mug to hold it in an upright position until it is set.

tip

When you are drying any piece of icing, place it on a piece of foam – both sides can then dry at the same time.

5 To complete, take the hearts with dusted edges and place a dab of royal icing behind them. Position them on the front of the cake top with one heart overlapping the other. You can than pipe the initials of the couple on the hearts or you could have embossed them whilst the hearts are still soft. To complete, add little flowers on wires in between the hearts.

lace flowers and hearts – flower paste

Both of these tops are a variation on the same theme, so when you have followed the lace flower instructions you will be able to make the heart design. The lace flower top matches the cake on page 31.

You will need
- Flower cutters, edible glitter, 20g wire, foam, royal icing, 28g wire, florist tape and ribbon.

Lace flower

1 For the lace flowers, use a selection of sizes of the flower cutters in the set and cut out two flowers per wire.

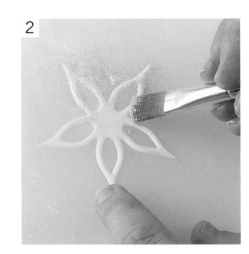

2 Leave to dry and decorate to match the flowers on the cake (see page 31).

3 Take a white 20g wire and cut it in half. (The flowers are heavy when finished, so do not try to use a thinner wire.) Turn a flower over and place it on a piece of foam face down; lay the wire on the back. Fill a piping (decorating) bag with royal icing, then squeeze a little royal icing around the wire. Leave to dry.

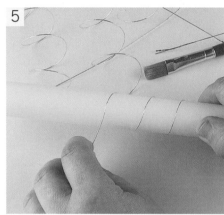

4 Place a few dots of royal icing on the other petals of the flower and lay another flower head back-to-back with the first one. Make sure the petals now alternate and are not lying on top of each other. You need three of these flowers for a good effect.

5 Now, using 28g silver or gold wire, curl the wire around a small rolling pin. You can use as many or as few as you wish, but nine to twelve strands look the best.

6 To assemble, tape together a flower, some lengths of ribbon and some of the curled wires with florist tape. Repeat this with all three flowers.

7 Place the flowers close to each other in a little triangle and position on the cake.

Hearts

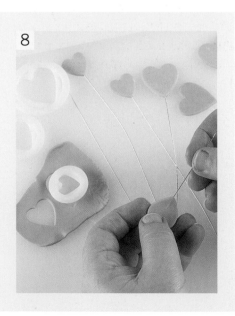

8 Roll the flower paste out a little thicker than for the lace flowers and cut out a series of hearts. Insert a 28g silver or gold wire into the point of each heart.

9 To complete this cake top we have used glass wired beads instead of curled wires. Continue as for the flower cake top.

old-fashioned toy box – pastillage

You will need

- Pastillage, paste colours, no. 1 piping tube (nozzle), scrap sugarpaste, foam, sugar glue, 20g wire and royal icing.

1 For this cake top you need to make your pastillage, then give it a wood effect by marbling it using brown and caramel colours. The colours will vary depending on what shade you want your box, or you could make it in a solid colour.

2 Roll out the pastillage and cut out the required box pieces – four rectangles 7.5 x 5cm (3 x 2in) and two 5cm (2in) squares. This makes a small box. I find a pizza wheel is best for this as it does not drag the paste. Roll out the leftover paste slightly thicker, cut a 7.5cm (3in) square and cut this in half to make two triangles. Leave all the shapes to dry on a piece

of foam – make sure that as you move them you keep the shape perfectly. You can enlarge this box easily or change its shape to a square one.

3 When the pieces are dry, make sure their edges are smooth by rubbing an emery board over them, but do be gentle. Make yourself a small quantity of royal icing in a colour to match the box and place in a small bag with a no. 1 tube in it.

4 Place one 7.5 x 5cm (3 x 2in) rectangle on a flat surface. This will be the base of your box. Now, place one of the 5cm (2in) squares against the base for the back of the box. Hold it in place with a small upright glass

or container, and pipe a small snail's trail along the base of the box to hold them together, making sure the back

is straight. Leave to dry. Do the same for one of the sides, using a rectangle.

5 Once this is dry, position the other square piece at the side of the box and pipe along the bottom, again making sure it is being held in the correct position with a glass. Place the front on and pipe the sides and base. This is slightly more difficult as you have to get your tube inside the box to pipe. Once the box is dry, half fill it with old bits of sugarpaste. It doesn't matter if you use different colours as this will be a base for the toys to sit on.

6 Take the lid of the box and hold it against the back of the box in an upright position. Pipe a small snail's trail to join the two pieces together, then place your two paste triangles or a long piece of foam on the side of

the box to act as wedges to support the lid. The further in you place the triangles, the more open the lid, so you can choose the position to suit whatever you are making to put in there. Remove the wedges when the royal icing is dry. I always keep my wedges so I don't have to make them each time.

tip

I have made this teddy to a size in keeping to the toy box, but if it is made on a larger scale it makes an ideal decoration for a christening cake or for a first birthday cake, and the beauty of models is you can make them a long time in advance.

7 To complete the box, pipe around the joins with a snail's trail on the outside of the box. This can easily be made into a trunk for a bon voyage cake – use a blossom cutter to make little pieces for the corners to look like reinforcement, dampen the back and stick over each base corner.

Now you need to make some small toys for the box. You can always make these in advance and leave them to dry. All of the toys are made in sugarpaste or modelling paste.

8 **Ball** – Make two spheres in two different colours both equal in size. Cut each ball in half with a sharp knife so as not to distort the ball too much, then cut each in half again. Now take two of each colour and alternate them so that the same colour is opposite each other. You will find they will stick back together without any glue. Finish off by re-rolling the sphere in your hands. It makes a great colourful ball.

9 **Teddy** – Start by making a sphere for the body and a smaller sphere for the head. Make two arms and two legs starting with a little

8

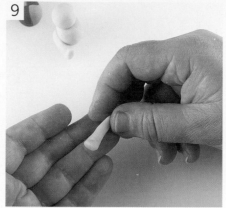

9

is for the boiler. Give your train little chimneys, boiler door etc and a roof over the driver cab. Pipe or paint on the entrance to the cab and paint on windows. Place three little wheels either side. For the rest of the carriages, roll out a little paste and give each carriage a roof. Add two wheels on either side. Stick all the pieces together with sugar glue.

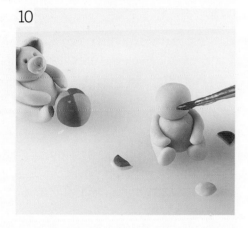

10

spacers and press them against the sides, then simply go over the top with a smoother, this will flatten the top and bottom. You may find you have excess paste that you need to trim, if so trim and smooth again. You will end up with a long square piece of paste; all you need to do now is cut it up into little bricks with the pizza wheel or sharp knife and place some in the toy box. Use different colours for the best effect.

14 If you want the train to look properly joined up then it becomes inedible. Paint a 20g white wire cut to length and thread the middle carriages onto the wire. The end carriage is just pushed part way on and so is the engine. Pipe a dot of royal icing at the point the wire enters the train just to hold it in place. If the train is on a wire you can have it bent over the toy box so it is hanging out.

cylinder and bending the ends over slightly for the teddy's feet. Put little pads in a colour on the base of the feet and on the paws.

10 For the nose make a small sphere and flatten with a smaller flattened sphere glued in place on top of that. Paint on two eyes and for the ears make a small sphere, flatten and cut in half. Repeat with another colour and make slightly smaller, then glue this to the ear so it looks the inside of the ear.

11 **Building bricks** – Roll your sugarpaste into a sausage. Place the sausage between marzipan

12 **Train** – Keep this to nice bright colours. Start by rolling out your sugarpaste to approx 2cm (³⁄₄in) in thickness and cut small rectangles all the same size for the carriages. For the engine make another rectangle the same size but then cut it in half widthways so you have two identical rectangles.

13 For the base of the engine, use the two half rectangles. Stand up one half rectangle at one end of the other half rectangle to make the driver's part of the engine. Now roll a small sausage and cut a piece to sit on the half rectangle at the front, this

14

parasol – flower paste or pastillage

of edible glue in the centre. Lay the second layer on the top so the petals go in between the petals on the first flower. Make a small hole for a wire to go through at a later stage and leave it to dry. You can use a variety of cutters for this cake top, but it is good to be able to utilize the cutters used elsewhere, then you realize that your cutters become multifunctional.

3 Roll a thin strip of paste – to get it fine and without marks from your fingers, try using your smoother to roll the paste. This makes a perfect sausage. Cut a length of approximately 10cm (4in) and curl one end for the handle of the parasol. Take a length of 24g white wire

You will need

■ Half-sphere former, flower paste or pastillage, flower cutters, 24g wire, royal icing and no. 1 piping tube.

1 For this you need a former in the shape of a half-sphere – an apple tray is good. Roll out your paste and with the largest of the lace flower cutters cut two layers.

2 Lay the first flower in the mould and squeeze a small amount

approximately 5cm (2in) long, and insert it into the straight bit of the handle and leave to dry. To assemble, use a bag of royal icing with a no. 1 tube and place a dot of icing around the wire at the top of the handle, thread this through the hole in the parasol top. You need only a small bit of wire coming through. Leave it upside down to dry on foam, then the tip of wire will sink into that. When it

3

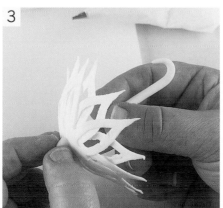

is dry, turn it over and place a little tip over the wire to complete the basics of the parasol.

4 To finish it off I have piped small loops on mine, but you could just use dots or leave it plain. This looks lovely and dainty in the centre of a cake for a female, with a few flowers coming from underneath it.

6 wedding cakes

techniques

Tiered wedding cakes are not as difficult to make as people think. Once you have mastered the art of cake decorating and you are happy with single cakes, you can certainly go on to tier a cake. When you make a sponge wedding cake, I would recommend you double-ice your cake – this gives the same effect as if you had a layer of marzipan on a fruit cake. A double layer also helps with stability. The first layer is only a thin coat; leave it to dry, then apply your second coat.

size of wedding cakes

The size of the tiers must be proportionate so that you achieve the correct shape. The shape you are after is a pyramid. To achieve this, the best sizes to go for are: 15cm (6in), 20cm (8in) and 25cm (10in) or 15cm (6in), 23cm (9in) and 30cm (12in) or 18cm (7in), 23cm (9in) and 28cm (11in). Your boards should never be bigger than the tier below, the only exception to when you can go slightly bigger is when you are using a stand and the tiers are not sitting directly above each other.

Never go larger than 18cm (7in) on the top tier. Otherwise it will look as if you have actually forgotten the top tier. For a two-tier, choose the top two tiers of the three tier sizes, not the bottom two, as these would look just too big and not so pleasing to the eye.

If you need to go as large as a four-tier, you need to use a 15cm (6in), 20cm (8in), 25cm (10in) and 30cm (12in) combination of cakes. Use the chart on page 139 for the number of portions you will get from these sizes. Just remember if you need more portions you do not need to make the wedding cake larger; make a cutting cake which is iced to match the main wedding cake but is not decorated. This is kept in the catering kitchen and can be sliced with the main cake. As it is iced nobody will know that the cake is not from the main wedding cake.

cake stands

This is the easiest method of displaying a wedding cake, and stands can be hired from all good sugarcraft shops. All you have to do is position the cakes on the stands, starting with the largest one first on the base. With a stand you can use any combination of fruit or sponge cake. Stands are both versatile and practical to use, and take away all the worry you first experience when you know you need to pillar and dowel a wedding cake, as all you can think about is, "Will it hold?"

Never remove just the bottom tier as that helps to keep the stability of the complete cake. Stands come in two, three or four tiers, and there is a huge variety of designs to choose from. They can be decorated with ribbons or in a material to match the bride's dress. The material can be all ruffled up over the stand and this all fits in with the planned colour scheme of the wedding. The effect the material gives is very delicate.

dowelling for pillars and stacking

If you use cake pillars or separators, or you stack a cake, you have to use cake dowels to support the weight of the cake. You can purchase plastic dowels in various lengths from sugarcraft shops. They come in white or clear plastic.

For cake pillars, insert the dowel down the cake pillar and through the cake. With a small sharp knife, mark the top point on each of the dowels. Remove one dowel at a time and, with a small hacksaw, just cut across it twice. You will then find you can snap the dowel to give a clean break. Insert the dowel back into the pillar and cake, and it should fit perfectly. Repeat with each of the others.

Cake pillars come in a variety of sizes and shapes; a 9cm (3.5in) is the most standard size for a three-tier cake. The shape depends on personal preference. A square pillar can really only be used on a square cake, but a round can be used on any of the shapes such as petal, oval, round. The hexagonal pillar can be also used on any shape cake and does give a soft pleasing finish to the cake.

For royal-iced cakes, if you have applied at least three coats of royal icing it will be strong enough to take the weight of the other tiers. Position your pillars on the cake as you would for sugarpaste (rolled fondant or ready-to-roll icing) cakes and just place your second tier on the pillars. Now repeat with the third.

Never cluster dowels in the centre of a tiered cake as it means all the weight is concentrated in one area. If you position the dowels as per the diagrams below you can spread out the weight. For square cakes, position the dowels in a rectangular or square shape 4cm (1½in) from the edges of the cake. For round cakes, position them in a triangular shape 4cm (1½in) from the edges of the cake.

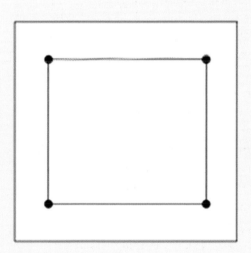

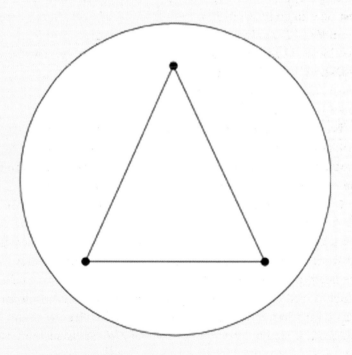

Separators

There are many different cake separators on the market to choose from. Alternatively you can use anything from candlesticks, to champagne glasses and tumblers. You do still, however, need to dowel the cake. Insert the dowel into the cake and this time cut the dowel off level with the cake. If you do find you have cut one slightly proud of the cake,

then remove the dowel from the cake (you may find you need a pair of tweezers to help you do this). You can just rub the end of the dowel on a piece of rough sandpaper to smooth the end. Then insert it back into the cake. The separator will sit on top of the dowel perfectly and support the weight of the other tiers.

One of the most popular separators at the moment is a simple

polystyrene cake dummy approximately 5cm (2in) in height, used with a ribbon tied around it. A thin cake card needs to be glued to the base of the dummy so that the cake card sits on the dowels. The picture aboves shows you a selection of cake stands and separators from angled tiers to cherubs. There is now a cake separator on the market to suit everyone's taste.

stacked cakes

Stacked cakes, where two or more cakes are placed directly on top of one another, are a popular style which originated in the United States. Many people believe stacked cakes do not need dowelling; however, they do still need the support, unless you have a royal-iced version.

You dowel the same as for the cake separators. Just position one cake directly on the cake below. The middle and top tier cakes must, however, be on 4mm (¼in) boards and it is the board that rests on the cake dowels. When you have stacked all the individually iced tiers, you need to either pipe around the base of each one or secure each tier with a little royal icing, then finish off with a ribbon round each tier. You can see the delightful effects that can be achieved with a stacked cake. Do be a little careful if you are using all sponge cake and not fruit, and make sure that your dowels go into the cake straight and not at a slight angle.

You need to remember only the top side of a cake board is of a food-grade quality. I would therefore recommend you place a piece of greaseproof (waxed) paper cut to fit on the underside of the board between each tier. Alternatively you can glue a second thin cake card back to back with the board the cake is sitting on so that there is a food grade side touching both cakes.

pros and cons of fresh flowers

Cake decorators have a variety of views as to whether fresh flowers should be used on a cake.

If we make a cake that requires fresh flowers, I always make sure the bride arranges for her florist to add them. This ensures the flowers match the wedding scheme and that way I have nothing to do with them.

However, in general I would not recommend using fresh flowers. When you make a cake you have such strict hygiene rules and regulations to apply, from kitchen conditions and where it is made, to the freshness of ingredients used, to ensure the cake is of a high standard. Then fresh flowers that have been sprayed with all sorts of insecticides are placed on the cake. They drop pollen and wilt unless somehow you can have them in water, but again I would not recommend this on a cake.

The other thing cake decorators should consider is that they cannot see the completed job. It is so much nicer seeing a cake being taken out which is fully decorated, than one that is just plainly iced.

Fresh flowers are, however, a personal choice, and I know a lot of people who would disagree with me. Fresh flowers will always continue to be used and are a cheaper option than handmade sugar flowers.

As an example, the picture shown on page 131 is of a modern, popular design of cake which uses fresh flowers. The flowers on the top can have bear grass loops put in among them to give an added dimension. The cake has a simple dot design over each tier.

cake designs

In this section I have made a variety of wedding cakes all using the basic principles of cake decorating that have been described throughout the book.

black spot flower

This stunning black cake is so easy to make and it is created using same principle as the Caterpillar cake (see page 28). Each tier is separated by a 5cm (2in) deep polystyrene cake dummy separator, which you can get specially made from most sugarcraft shops. I placed black ribbon around the side of each dummy and a gateau board is stuck to the base of each using a little royal icing. The bottom two cakes are dowelled and a dummy is placed on top of both. The flowers are positioned around the cakes and hide the dummy separators from view.

lace flower cake

In the sugarpaste section we gave details for making this cake as a single tier (see page 31) and gave instructions for the cake top on page 116. As a three-tier it gives a stunning look; all the tiers have been decorated with matching 3mm (⅛in) ribbon running round it and the same design used on all the three tiers, the amount of decoration increasing as the tiers get larger. Each tier is joined with a small line of shell piping, then the cake top is placed in position to complete this stunning cake. The matching lace flower cake top complements it well and adds some drama and height.

tiered chocolate cake

This three-tiered round cake has been coated in chocolate sugarpaste (rolled fondant or ready-to-roll icing); the ribbon strips are made of two colours of modelling chocolate. Cut the strips out with a pizza cutter, then roll them up. This makes the strips easier to handle. Dampen the cake where the ribbon strip is going be to placed and, starting at the back, place the strip around the cake.

The bow for this cake is made in a slightly different way to any others in the book. Roll out your paste, keeping the same design running through it. Use an oval cutter to cut two large ovals and one small oval. Fold each oval in half to make a loop and, if it needs it, stick them with a dab of water. Place both loops on the cake and finish off the centre of the bow with a small oval.

To complete this cake I have simply finished it off with three white chocolate lilies, remembering the rule about keeping to an odd number of decorations.

Chocolate is so popular these days and this simple stacked cake with a sugar bow and finished off with piped dots and chocolate lilies looks absolutely stunning.

curly wire cake

This cake brings together everything shown in this book. As this design is very difficult to make a template for, we have plain-iced a three-tier cake. Dowel the base tier, then place the second tier directly on the base. Join them with a small line of snail's trail piping and leave to dry.

Place your cakes on a tilting turntable for ease when piping this side design. Pipe scrolls, with a no. 1.5 tube (nozzle), all around the lower half of the bottom tier of the cake in the same colour as you iced your cakes. It is piped freehand and the pattern is quite random, but do keep it so it all comes up to the same level. Leave to dry and pipe the top tier in the same way, but do not worry about each tier being absolutely identical in design.

When the tiers are dry, sit and paint the scroll work with your chosen colour, in our case gold. You may, however, leave the cake with the piping left unpainted.

Dowel the second tier so it supports your chosen separator. We are using a Perspex tube separator and filled it with curled wire to match the side design on the cake.

For the cake top we have again used curly wire, with feathers and glass beads, all wired into a decoration that just sits into a posy pic. This makes for an eye-catching and elaborate-looking cake.

cupcakes

For weddings, individual cakes are very fashionable, so cupcakes are used more and more. This is still quite a new idea where you can have cupcakes for each individual person made in a colour scheme to match a wedding. You can vary the cakes flavours so that some are chocolate, others sponge; even carrot cake can be made this way. The list is endless. To ice the top you can either just use a frosting or you can cut the tops level, then lay a disc of sugarpaste (rolled fondant or ready-to-roll icing) on the top, as in the picture. Just finish the tops off with a design of the bride's choice. It does not have to be flowers. Again, with the use of cutters, you can do cut-out work on each, which looks very effective. I have made some cupcakes and flat-iced them, displaying them in the smallest cupcake stand. They are decorated using unwired roses and it is very easy to create a fantastic display.

The downside to a cake like this is that it all has to be made at the last minute, so do make sure you allow yourself the time.

You can get six-tier cupcake stands which you can fit 100 to 120 cupcakes on, and they do create the same impact as a traditional wedding cake does. I have used silver cupcake cases to add that touch of sophistication to my cupcake display.

The other alternative to cupcakes is individual miniature cakes; they are then given to the guests to take home. You can get tins (pans) to make the individual cakes in, but they are fiddly to ice and decorate and can be a lot more time-consuming than a big wedding cake.

With this option there is not a cake for the bride and groom to cut. Some don't worry about that and instead have their picture taken feeding each other with a small cake, while others choose to have a 15cm (6in) or 18cm (7in) small cake that can be cut up. This can be the fruit cake option if they choose.

7 the essentials

storage and transportation

Always store cakes in cake boxes that fit the size of your boards. You can find cake boxes at any sugarcraft or cook shop, and they will keep your cakes dust-free while still allowing them to breathe. Try to leave cakes in out-of-the-way places that are neither too warm nor too cold; room temperature is ideal. Never, ever store them in the kitchen. The fluctuating temperatures and steam will quickly ruin all of your hard work.

Before you transport cakes, set them in cake boxes and seal the lids with masking or adhesive tape to prevent them from flying off. Never place cakes on the front or back seat of your car. Car seats are sloped, so there is very little to stop your cake from sailing onto the floor if you have to brake suddenly. It is much better to set cakes on towels, blankets or non-slip matting, which you can find at any sugarcraft or cook shop, in the boot (trunk) of your car. Surround them with rolled-up towels to prevent them from shifting and to protect them from any other items that you might be storing in the boot.

cutting cakes

The standard fruit-cake portion for one person is 2.5cm (1in) squared. For a sponge cake, the standard portion is 5cm x 2.5cm squared (2in x 1in squared). The diagrams on the right show the best ways of cutting round and square cakes. When you cut the portions, be sure to use a good-quality sharp knife without too much "flex".

If you are preparing to cut a cake that has been covered using the all-in-one method, first slide a sharp knife round the base of the cake to free it from the board. This will make it much easier to lift and serve the portions later.

Cutting round and square cakes

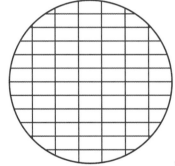

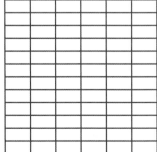

tip

If you know you are going to use only part of a cake, cut it straight down the middle. Slice equal-sized portions from the inner sides of both halves. Then, when you are finished, push what remains of the two halves together to prevent them from drying out.

portion guide

The following tables will help you to determine how many servings a cake will produce.

Round and square cakes

Fruit	Round/all other shapes except number and novelty cakes	Square	Sponge	Round/all other shapes except number and novelty cakes	Square
13cm (5in)	16	25	13cm (5in)	8	12
15cm (6in)	25	36	15cm (6in)	12	18
18cm (7in)	36	49	18cm (7in)	18	24
20cm (8in)	49	64	20cm (8in)	24	32
23cm (9in)	64	84	23cm (9in)	32	42
25cm (10in)	84	100	25cm (10in)	42	50
28cm (11in)	100	121	28cm (11in)	50	61
30cm (12in)	120	144	30cm (12in)	61	72
36cm (14¼in)	144	196	36cm (14¼in)	72	98
41cm (16¼in)	196	256	41cm (16¼in)	98	128

Number cakes

Fruit		Sponge	
Number 0	40	Number 0	20
Number 1	30	Number 1	15
Numbers 2–9	40	Numbers 2–9	20

Novelty cakes

Fruit/Sponge

Most novelty fruit cakes produce 50 portions, while novelty sponge cakes produce 25 to 30 portions. These numbers may sound impressive at first, but remember that novelty cakes are much shallower than those baked in ordinary tins (pans).

Marzipan guide

This table will help you to work out how much marzipan you need to cover your cake.

Round and square cakes

Fruit	Round/all other shapes except number and novelty cakes	Square
13cm (5in)	275g (9½oz)	375g (13oz)
15cm (6in)	375g (13oz)	750g (1lb 10oz)
18cm (7in)	750g (1lb 10oz)	875g (2lb)
20cm (8in)	875g (2lb)	1kg (2lb 4oz)
23cm (9in)	1kg (2lb 4oz)	1.25kg (2lb 12oz)
25cm (10in)	1.25kg (2lb 12oz)	1.5kg (3lb 5oz)
28cm (11in)	1.5kg (3lb 5oz)	1.75kg (3lb 13oz)
30cm (12in)	1.75kg (3lb 13oz)	2kg (4lb 8oz)
36cm (14¼in)	2kg (4lb 8oz)	2.5kg (5lb 8oz)
41cm (16¼in)	2.5kg (5lb 8oz)	3kg (6lb 8oz)

Number cakes

Fruit/Sponge	
Number 0	1kg (2lb 4oz)
Number 1	875g (2lb)
Numbers 2–9	1kg (2lb 4oz)

Novelty cakes

Fruit/Sponge

You will need 1kg (2lb 4oz) of marzipan to cover most novelty cakes.

Sugarpaste guide

This table will help you to work out how much sugarpaste (rolled fondant or ready-to-roll icing) you need to cover your cake.

Round and square cakes

	Round/all other shapes except number and novelty cakes	Square
13cm (5in)	375g (13oz)	500g (1lb 2oz)
15cm (6in)	500g (1lb 2oz)	875g (2lb)
18cm (7in)	875g (2lb)	1kg (2lb 4oz)
20cm (8in)	1kg (2lb 4oz)	1.25kg (2lb 12oz)
23cm (9in)	1.25kg (2lb 12oz)	1.5kg (3lb 5oz)
25cm (10in)	1.5kg (3lb 5oz)	1.75kg (3lb 13oz)
28cm (11in)	1.75kg (3lb 13oz)	2kg (4lb 8oz)
30cm (12in)	2kg (4lb 8oz)	2.5kg (5lb 8oz)
36cm (14¼in)	2.5kg (5lb 8oz)	3kg (6lb 8oz)
41cm (16¼in)	3kg (6lb 8oz)	3.5kg (8lb)

Number cakes

Fruit/Sponge	
Number 0	1.25kg (2lb 12oz)
Number 1	1kg (2lb 4oz)
Numbers 2–9	1.25kg (2lb 12oz)

Novelty cakes

Fruit/Sponge

You will need 1.25kg (2lb 12oz) of sugarpaste to cover most novelty cakes.

recipes

In this section, ingredient quantities are given for 15cm (6in) round/12.5cm (5in) square cakes through to 32cm (13in) round/30cm (12in) square cakes for both the classic fruit and sponge cake recipes. For most variations of these recipes, however, ingredient quantities are only given for 13cm (5in) round/10cm (4in) square cakes to 20cm (8in) round/18cm (7in) square cakes. That is because these cakes are prone to flopping if they are made any larger. If you are baking for a large group, simply make more cakes, rather than increasing the sizes of the individual cakes.

fruit cakes

Round/square cakes

Round	15cm (6in)	18cm (7in)	20cm (8in)	23cm (9in)	25cm (10in)	28cm (11in)	30cm (12in)	32cm (13in)
Square	13cm (5in)	15cm (6in)	18cm (7in)	20cm (8in)	23cm (9in)	25cm (10in)	28cm (11in)	30cm (12in)
Glacé (candied) cherries, chopped	40g (1½oz/3 tbsp)	65g (2½oz/4 tbsp)	75g (2¾oz/⅓ cup)	100g (3½oz/½ cup)	150g (5½oz/¾ cup)	225g (8oz/1 cup)	300g (10½oz/1¼ cups)	350g (12oz/1½ cups)
Currants	150g (5½oz/1 cup)	220g (8oz/1¼ cups)	350g (12oz/2 cups)	450g (1lb/3½ cups)	625g (1lb 7oz/5 cups)	775g (1lb 12oz/5¾ cups)	1.2kg (2lb 10oz/10¾ cups)	1.4kg (3lb 5oz/11¼ cups)
Sultanas (golden raisins)	50g (1¾oz/¼ cup)	90g (3¼oz/½ cup)	125g (4½oz/¾ cup)	200g (7oz/1¼ cups)	225g (8oz/1½ cups)	375g (13oz/1¾ cups)	400g (14oz/2¼ cups)	500g (1lb 2oz/3¾ cups)
Raisins	50g (1¾oz/¼ cup)	90g (3¼oz/½ cup)	125g (4½oz/¾ cup)	200g (7oz/1¼ cups)	225g (8oz/1½ cups)	375g (13oz/1¾ cups)	400g (14oz/2¼ cups)	500g (1lb 2oz/3¾ cups)
Mixed fruit peel	25g (1oz/¼ cup)	50g (1¾oz/⅓ cup)	50g (1¾oz/⅓ cup)	75g (2¾oz/½ cup)	100g (3½oz/¾ cup)	150g (5½oz/1 cup)	200g (7oz/1¼ cups)	250g (9oz/1¾ cups)
Lemon rind, grated	½ lemon	½ lemon	1 lemon	1 lemon	1 lemon	2 lemons	2 lemons	2 lemons
Plain (all-purpose) flour	100g (3½oz/ ¾ cup)	175g (6oz/ 1½ cups)	200g (7oz/ 1⅔ cups)	350g (12oz/ 3 cups)	400g (14oz/ 3½ cups)	600g (1lb 5oz/ 5¼ cups)	700g (1lb 9oz/ 6¼ cups)	825g (1lb 14oz/ 7½ cups)
Almonds, chopped	25g (1oz/¼ cup)	50g (1¾oz/½ cup)	50g (1¾oz/½cup)	50g (1¾oz/½ cup)	100g (3½oz/1 cup)	150g (5½oz/1½ cups)	200g (7oz/2 cups)	250g (9oz/2¼ cups)
Ground cinnamon	¼ tsp	¼ tsp	¾ tsp	1 tsp	1¼ tsp	1¼ tsp	1½ tsp	1¾ tsp
Nutmeg	¼ tsp	¼ tsp	½ tsp	½ tsp	1 tsp	1 tsp	1¼ tsp	1¼ tsp
Mixed (pumpkin pie) spice	¼ tsp	¼ tsp	¼ tsp	½ tsp	1 tsp	1 tsp	1¼ sp	1¼ tsp
Butter/ margarine	75g (2¾oz/ ⅓ cup)	150g (5½oz/ ¾ cup)	175g (6oz/ ¾ cup)	275g (9½oz/ 1¼ cups)	350g (12oz/ 1½ cups)	500g (1lb 2oz/ 2¼ cups)	600g (1lb 5oz/ 2½ cups)	800g (1lb 12oz/ 3½ cups)
Soft brown sugar	75g (2¾ oz/ ½ cup)	150g (5½oz/ 1 cup)	175g (6oz/ 1¼ cups)	275g (9½oz/ 1¾ cups)	350g (12oz/ 2¼ cups)	500g (1lb 2oz/ 3 cups)	600g (1lb 5oz/ 3½ cups)	800g (1lb 12oz/ 4¾ cups)
Eggs	2	3	4	5	6	9	11	14
Black treacle (molasses)	1 tsp	1 tsp	1 tbsp	1 tbsp	1 tbsp	2 tbsp	2 tbsp	2 tbsp
Approximate baking time at 120°C/250°F/Gas Mark ½	2 hours	2½ hours	3 hours	3¼ hours	3¾ hours	4½ hours	5½ hours	6½ hours

Fruit cake

Fruit cake is rather high-maintenance after baking, requiring a big "drink" of alcoholic mixture – drizzle 60ml (4 tbsp) over a 20cm (8in) cake – immediately after it comes out of the oven, followed by a series of smaller "drinks" – drizzle over roughly 15ml (3 tbsp) – every one to two weeks thereafter. If you are short of time and need a fruit cake quickly, wrap it in greaseproof (waxed) paper after you have fed it and it has cooled down, and put it in the freezer. Freeze the cake for a minimum of 24 hours, then defrost it at room temperature for another 24 hours at least. Once the cake has defrosted, you can continue with the marzipan stage.

Method

1. Put the cherries in a mixing bowl with the currants, sultanas, raisins, mixed fruit peel and lemon rind.
2. In a separate bowl, blend the plain flour, almonds, ground cinnamon, nutmeg and mixed spice.
3. Cream the margarine until it is light, fluffy and white in colour. Add the brown sugar and mix a little further.
4. Add the eggs, one at a time, to the butter, with a little of the flour mixture.
5. Stir in the remaining flour mixture and the dried fruit.
6. Add the black treacle and blend.
7. Spoon the mixture into a lined tin (pan) and make a slight depression in the centre of the mixture. This helps to keep the cake level as it bakes.
8. After baking, feed the cake and wrap it in two layers of greaseproof paper and store it in a plastic bag or airtight container for three months.

Gluten-free fruit cake

If you would like to make this fruit cake even richer, increase the quantity of dried fruit and cherries used to taste.

Round/Square Cakes				
Round	13cm	15cm	18cm	20cm
	(5in)	(6in)	(7in)	(8in)
Square	10cm	13cm	15cm	18cm
	(4in)	(5in)	(6in)	(7in)
Water/apple or	70ml	125ml	190ml	250ml
pineapple juice	(5 tbsp)	(8 tbsp)	(7fl oz/1 cup)	(9fl oz/1 cup)
Soft brown/white sugar	25g	55g	85g	115g
	(1oz/¼ cup)	(2oz/½ cup)	(3oz/¾ cup)	(4oz/1 cup)
Vegetable margarine	175g	225g	350g	450g
(shortening)	(6oz/¾ cup)	(8oz/1 cup)	(12oz/1½ cups)	(1lb/2 cups)
Dried fruit	175g	225g	350g	450g
	(6oz/1 cup)	(8oz/1½ cups)	(12oz/1¾ cups)	(1lb/3 cups)
Glacé (candied)	25g	40g	55g	55g
cherries	(1oz/3 tbsp)	(1½oz/3 tbsp)	(2oz/½ cup)	(2oz/½ cup)
Gluten-free flour	70g	85g	150g	200g
	(2½oz/9 tbsp)	(3oz/⅔ cup)	(5½oz/1¼ cups)	(7oz/1⅔ cups)
Mixed (pumpkin pie) spice	¼ tsp	½ tsp	¾ tsp	1 tsp
Ground almonds	40g	55g	85g	85g
	(1½oz/¼ cup)	(2oz/½ cup)	(3oz/¾ cup)	(3oz/¾ cup)
Eggs	1	1	2	2
Approximate baking time at 120ºC/250ºF/Gas Mark ½				
	45mins	60mins	75mins	90mins

method

1. Put the water/apple or pineapple juice, brown/white sugar, vegetable margarine, dried fruit and glacé cherries in a pan and boil.
2. Continue boiling for approximately 10 minutes, then remove the mixture from the heat and leave it to cool.
3. Blend in the gluten-free flour, mixed spice, ground almonds and eggs, plus a little more water/fruit juice if necessary to soften the mixture.
4. Spoon the mixture into a lined tin (pan), then use the spoon to create a slight depression in the centre of the mixture. This helps to keep the cake level as it bakes.

Egg-free fruit cake

If you would like to make this fruit cake even richer, increase the quantity of dried fruit and cherries used to taste.

Round/square cakes				
Round	13cm	15cm	18cm	20cm
	(5in)	(6in)	(7in)	(8in)
Square	10cm	13cm	15cm	18cm
	(4in)	(5in)	(6in)	(7in)
Water/apple or Pineapple juice	70ml	125ml	190ml	250ml
	(5 tbsp)	(8 tbsp)	(7 fl oz/1 cup)	(9 fl oz/1 cup)
Soft brown/white sugar	25g	55g	85g	115g
	(1oz/¼ cup)	(2oz/½ cup)	(3oz/¾ cup)	(4oz/1 cup)
Vegetable margarine (shortening)	175g	225g	350g	450g
	(6oz/¾ cup)	(8oz/1 cup)	(12oz/1½ cups)	(1lb/2 cups)
Dried fruit	175g	225g	350g	450g
	(6oz/1 cup)	(8oz/1½ cups)	(12oz/1¾ cups)	(1lb/3 cups)
Glacé (candied) cherries	25g	40g	55g	55g
	(1oz/3 tbsp)	(1½oz/3 tbsp)	(2oz/½ cup)	(2oz/½ cup)
Self-raising (self-rising) flour	55g	85g	175g	225g
	(2oz/½cup)	(3oz/⅔ cup)	(6oz/1½ cups)	(8oz/2 cups)
Mixed (pumpkin pie) spice	1.25ml	2.5ml	5ml	5ml
	(¼ tsp)	(½ tsp)	(1 tsp)	(1 tsp)
Ground almonds (optional)	25g	40g	55g	55g
	(1oz/¼ cup)	(1½oz/¼ cup)	(2oz/½ cup)	(2oz/½ cup)
Approximate baking time at 120°C/250°F/Gas Mark ½				
	45mins	60mins	75mins	90mins

method

1. Put the water/apple or pineapple juice, brown/white sugar, vegetable margarine, dried fruit and glacé cherries in a pan and boil.

2. Continue boiling for approximately 10 minutes, then remove the mixture from the heat and leave it to cool.

3. Blend in the self-raising flour, mixed spice and ground almonds, if used, plus a little more water/fruit juice if necessary to soften the mixture.

4. Spoon the mixture into a lined tin (pan), then use the spoon to create a slight depression in the centre of the mixture. This helps to keep the cake level as it bakes.

Dairy-free fruit cake

Make the fruit cake recipe (see ingredient quantities, page 141) dairy-free by substituting vegetable margarine for the ordinary margarine.

Diabetic fruit cake

If you would like to make this fruit cake even richer, increase the quantity of dried fruit and cherries used to taste.

Diabetic fruit cake

Round/square cakes				
Round	13cm	15cm	18cm	20cm
	(5in)	(6in)	(7in)	(8in)
Square	10cm	13cm	15cm	18cm
	(4in)	(5in)	(6in)	(7in)
Plain (all-purpose) flour	85g	115g	140g	200g
	(3oz/⅔ cup)	(4oz/1 cup)	(5oz/1¼ cups)	(7oz/1⅔ cups)
Salt	¼ tsp	¼ tsp	½ tsp	½ tsp
Cinnamon	½ tsp	½ tsp	1 tsp	1 tsp
Mixed (pumpkin pie) spice	½ tsp	½ tsp	1 tsp	1 tsp
Nutmeg	½ tsp	½ tsp	½ tsp	½ tsp
Raisins	225g	200g	225g	280g
	(8oz/1½ cups)	(7oz/1¼ cups)	(8oz/1½cups)	(10oz/1¾ cups)
Currants	225g	200g	225g	280g
	(8oz/1¼ cups)	(7oz/1¼ cups)	(8oz/1¼ cups)	(10oz/1½ cups)
Sultanas (golden raisins)	225g	200g	225g	280g
	(8oz/1½ cups)	(7oz/1¼ cups)	(8oz/1½ cups)	(10oz/1¾ cups)
Glacé (candied) cherries	115g	85g	115g	175g
	(4oz/½ cup)	(3oz/⅓cup)	(4oz/½cup)	(6oz/¾ cup)
Flaked (slivered) almonds	115g	85g	115g	175g
	(4oz/1⅓ cups)	(3oz/1 cup)	(4oz/1⅓ cups)	(6oz/1½ cups)
Polyunsaturated margarine	140g	115g	140g	175g
	(5oz/½ cup)	(4oz/½ cup)	(5oz/½ cup)	(6oz/¾ cup)
Soft brown sugar	55g	115g	55g	55g
	(2oz/½ cup)	(4oz/1 cup)	(2oz/½ cup)	(2oz/½ cup)
Eggs	4	3	4	5
Bicarbonate of (baking) soda	½ tsp	¾ tsp	1 tsp	1½ tsp
Warm water	5ml	7.5ml	10ml	15ml
	(1 tsp)	(1½ tsp)	(2 tsp)	(1 tbsp)
Brandy (optional)	75ml	60ml	75ml	105ml
	(5 tbsp)	(4 tbsp)	(5 tbsp)	(7 tbsp)
Approximate baking time at 150°C/300°F/Gas Mark 2				
	90mins	120mins	150mins	180mins

method

1. In a mixing bowl, blend the plain flour, salt, cinnamon, mixed spice, nutmeg, raisins, currants, sultanas, glacé cherries and flaked almonds.

2. In a separate bowl, stir together the polyunsaturated margarine and soft brown sugar.

3. Gradually add the eggs and the dry ingredients from step 1 to the margarine mixture.

4. Dissolve the bicarbonate of soda in the warm water, then add this to the margarine mixture. To soften its consistency, add a little more water, 15ml (1 tbsp) at a time.

5. Spoon the mixture into a lined cake tin (pan) and level it. After baking, drizzle the fruit cake with the brandy, if used.

sponge cakes

Sponge cake

Round/square cakes								
Round	15cm (6in)	18cm (7in)	20cm (8in)	23cm (9in)	25cm (10in)	28cm (11in)	30cm (12in)	32cm (13in)
Square	13cm (5in)	15cm (6in)	18cm (7in)	20cm (8in)	23cm (9in)	25cm (10in)	28cm (11in)	30cm (12in)
Butter/ margarine	225g (8oz/1 cup)	275g (9½oz/1¼ cups)	336g (11½oz/1½ cups)	450g (1lb/2 cups)	616g (1lb 5oz/2½ cups)	700g (1lb 9oz/3 cups)	730g (1lb 10oz/3¼ cups)	787g (1lb 2oz/3½ cups)
Caster (superfine) sugar	225g (8oz/1 cup)	275g (9½oz/1¼cups)	336g (11½oz/1½cups)	450g (1lb/2¼ cups)	616g (1lb 5oz/2¾ cups)	700g (1lb 9oz/3 cups)	730g (1lb 10oz/3¼ cups)	787g (1lb 12oz/3½ cups)
Eggs	4	5	6	8	10	12	13	14
Self-raising (self-rising) flour	225g (8oz/2 cups)	275g (9½oz/2¼ cups)	336g (11½oz/3 cups)	450g (1lb/4 cups)	616g (1lb 5oz/51¼cups)	700g (1lb 9oz/6¼ cups)	730g (1lb 10oz/6½ cups)	787g (1lb 12oz/7 cups)
Milk/water	5ml (1 tsp)	5ml (1 tsp)	10ml (2 tsp)	10ml (2 tsp)	10ml (2 tsp)	20ml (4 tsp)	20ml (4 tsp)	30ml (2 tbsp)
Approximate baking time at 120°C/250°F/Gas Mark ½	40mins	40min sq/ 50mins rd	50mins	60mins	60mins sq/ 85mins rd	85mins	95mins	95mins

Number cakes

For sponge cakes baked in number 0 and 2–9 frames, use the ingredient quantities for the 15cm (6in) round/13cm (5in) square cake for a shallow cake, and the ingredient quantities for the 18cm (7in) round/15cm (6in) square cake for a deeper cake. For sponge cakes baked in a number 1 frame, use 175g (6oz) of all dry ingredients, 3 eggs and 5ml (1 tsp) milk or water. Bake number 1–5, 7 and 8 cakes for 40 minutes, and number 0, 6 and 9 cakes for 45 minutes.

Novelty cakes

For all sponge cakes baked in novelty tins (pans), use the ingredient quantities for either the 18cm (7in) round/15cm (6in) square cake or the 20cm (8in) round/18cm (7in) square cake. Using the latter guarantees a deeper cake.

method

1. In a mixing bowl, blend together the butter/margarine and the caster sugar until the mixture is light and fluffy.
2. Break the eggs into a separate mixing bowl and whisk them with a fork.
3. Alternately pour the eggs and the self-raising flour into the butter mixture, then fold together with a spoon.
4. Gradually add the milk/water to the mixture to soften its consistency.
5. Spoon the mixture into a lined tin (pan) and make a slight depression in the centre of the mixture. This helps to keep the cake level as it bakes.
6. After baking, use the cake immediately or freeze it either plain or buttercreamed for up to one month.

Sponge cake flavour variations

CHOCOLATE Blend 2 heaped tablespoons cocoa powder with the milk/water used in the sponge cake recipe (see ingredient quantities on page 145). For a marbled effect, make half of the sponge cake plain (see ingredient quantities on page 145) and half of it with chocolate flavouring. Add the two mixtures to the tin (pan) in alternate spoonfuls, then run a knife through the ingredients to create the marbling.

CHOCOLATE CHIP Add a handful of chocolate chips to the sponge cake recipe (see ingredient quantities on page 145).

COFFEE Blend 1 level tablespoon instant or liquid coffee with the milk/water used in the sponge cake recipe (see ingredient quantities on page 145). You could also add a handful of walnuts, if you like.

LEMON Add the grated rind and juice of 1 lemon to the sponge cake recipe (see ingredient quantities on page 145).

ORANGE Add the grated rind and juice of 1 orange to the sponge cake recipe (see ingredient quantities on page 145).

ST CLEMENT'S CAKE Add the grated rind and juice of both 1 orange and 1 lemon for a lovely St Clement's cake.

Gluten-free sponge cake

This cake should be cooked in two halves to prevent it from flopping. You will need two lined tins (pans) of the same size; if you have only one tin, halve the mixture and cook one half at a time.

Round/square cakes						
Round	15cm	18cm	20cm	23cm	25cm	28cm
	(6in)	(7in)	(8in)	(9in)	(10in)	(11in)
Square	13cm	15cm	18cm	20cm	23cm	25cm
	(5in)	(6in)	(7in)	(8in)	(9in)	(10in)
Gluten-free flour	150g	200g	250g	350g	425g	500g
	(5½oz/1½ cups)	(7oz/1⅔ cups)	(9oz/2¼ cups)	(12oz/3 cups)	(15oz/3⅔ cups)	(1lb 2oz/4½ cups)
Ground almonds	50g	50g	75g	100g	150g	175g
	(1¾oz/½ cup)	(1¾oz/½ cup)	(2¾oz/½ cup)	(3½oz/¾ cup)	(5½oz/1 cup)	(6oz/1¼ cups)
Vegetable margarine	200g	250g	350g	450g	600g	700g
(shortening)	(7oz/1 cup)	(9oz/1¼ cups)	(12oz/1½ cups)	(1lb/2¼ cups)	(1lb 5oz/2¾ cups)	(1lb 9oz/3 cups)
Caster (superfine)	200g	250g	350g	450g	600g	700g
sugar	(7oz/1 cup)	(9oz/1¼ cups)	(12oz/1¾ cups)	(1lb/2 cups)	(1lb 5oz/2½ cups)	(1lb 9oz/3 cups)
Eggs	4	5	6	8	10	12
Warm water (optional)						

Bake the cake for approximately 45 minutes at 120°C/250°F/Gas Mark ½.

method

1. Blend the gluten-free flour and ground almonds in a mixing bowl and set it aside.

2. In a separate bowl, cream the vegetable margarine and caster sugar until the mixture is light and creamy, and the colour has visibly lightened.

3. Scrape down the bowl and give the mixture one more quick stir, then gradually add the flour mixture and the eggs.

4. If necessary, add just enough warm water to soften the mixture.

Egg-free sponge cake

This cake should be cooked in two halves to prevent it from flopping. You will need two lined tins (pans) of the same size; if you have only one tin, halve the mixture and cook one half at a time.

Round/square cakes				
Round	13cm	15cm	18cm	20cm
	(5in)	(6in)	(7in)	(8in)
Square	10cm	13cm	15cm	18cm
	(4in)	(5in)	(6in)	(7in)
Vegetable margarine	25g	30g	40g	50g
(shortening)	(1oz/2 tbsp)	(1oz/2 tbsp)	(1½oz/¼ cup)	(1¾oz/¼ cup)
Sugar	50g	65g	80g	100g
	(1¾oz/¼ cup)	(2½oz/¼ cup)	(3oz/½ cup)	(3½oz/½ cup)
Golden (corn) syrup	50g	65g	80g	100g
	(1¾oz/¼ cup)	(2½oz/¼ cup)	(3oz/½ cup)	(3½oz/½ cup)
Bicarbonate of (baking) soda	¼ tsp	½ tsp	¾ tsp	1 tsp
Milk	125ml	150ml	200ml	300ml
	(4fl oz/½ cup)	(5fl oz/½ cup)	(7fl oz/1 cup)	(10fl oz/1¼ cups)
Self-raising (self-rising) flour	175g	230g	280g	350g
	(6oz/1½ cups)	(9oz/2¼ cups)	(10oz/2½ cups)	(12oz/3 cups)
Salt	to taste	to taste	to taste	to taste
Cocoa powder	25g	30g	40g	50g
	(1oz/¼ cup)	(1oz/¼ cup)	(1½oz/½ cup)	(1¾ oz/½ cup)
Approximate baking time at 190ºC/375ºF/Gas Mark 5				
	20mins	25mins	30mins	40mins

method

1. Cream together the vegetable margarine, sugar and golden syrup in a mixing bowl.
2. In a separate bowl, dissolve the bicarbonate of soda in the milk.
3. Blend the self-raising flour, salt and cocoa powder in another bowl, then alternately add the margarine and bicarbonate of soda mixtures. You should end up with a thick batter.
4. Divide the mixture equally between the two lined tins, then bake immediately.

Gluten-, dairy- and egg-free sponge cake

This cake should be cooked in two halves to prevent it from flopping. You will need two lined tins (pans) of the same size; if you have only one tin, halve the mixture and cook one half at a time.

Round/square cakes				
Round	13cm	15cm	18cm	20cm
	(5in)	(6in)	(7in)	(8in)
Square	10cm	13cm	15cm	18cm
	(4in)	(5in)	(6in)	(7in)
Dairy-free margarine	25g	30g	40g	50g
	(1oz/2 tbsp)	(1oz/2 tbsp)	(1½oz/¼ cup)	(1¾oz/¼ cup)
Sugar	50g	65g	80g	100g
	(1¾oz/¼ cup)	(2½oz/¼ cup)	(3oz/½ cup)	(3½oz/½ cup)
Golden (corn) syrup	50g	65g	80g	100g
	(1¾oz/¼ cup)	(2½oz/¼ cup)	(3oz/½ cup)	(3½oz/½ cup)
Bicarbonate of (baking) soda	1 tsp	1¼ tsp	1½ tsp	2 tsp
Soya milk	125ml	150ml	200ml	300ml
	(4fl oz/½ cup)	(5fl oz/½ cup)	(7fl oz/1 cup)	(10fl oz/1¼ cups)
Gluten-free flour	175g	230g	280g	350g
	(6oz/1½ cups)	(9oz/2¼ cups)	(10oz/2½ cups)	(12oz/3 cups)
Salt	to taste	to taste	to taste	to taste
Cocoa powder	25g	30g	40g	50g
(optional)	(½oz/¼ cup)	(1oz/¼ cup)	(1½oz/½ cup)	(1¾oz/½ cup)
Approximate baking time at 190°C/375°F/Gas Mark 5				
	20mins	25mins	30mins	40mins

method

1. Cream together the dairy-free margarine, sugar and golden syrup in a mixing bowl.
2. In a separate bowl, dissolve the bicarbonate of soda in the soya milk.
3. Blend the gluten-free flour, salt and cocoa powder, if used, in another bowl, then alternately add the margarine and bicarbonate of soda mixtures. You should end up with a thick batter.
4. Divide the mixture equally between the two lined tins, then bake immediately.

Dairy-free sponge cake

Make the sponge cake recipe (see ingredient quantities, page 145) dairy-free by substituting water for the milk, and vegetable margarine for the butter/ordinary margarine.

Dairy-free chocolate topping

If you wish to use this topping as a filling as well, double the quantity of all ingredients.

method

1. Break up the dairy-free plain (dark) chocolate and add it to a stainless-steel mixing bowl with the vegetable margarine and soya milk.

2. Set the bowl over a pan of boiling water and reduce the heat. Stir the mixture until it is completely melted.
4. Add the icing sugar and blend until smooth.
5. Apply to the cake immediately.

Dairy-free chocolate topping

Round/Square Cakes				
Round	13cm	15cm	18cm	20cm
	(5in)	(6in)	(7in)	(8in)
Square	10cm	13cm	15cm	18cm
	(4in)	(5in)	(6in)	(7in)
Dairy-free plain (dark) chocolate	25g	50g	75g	100g
	(1oz)	(1¾oz)	(2¾oz)	(3½oz)
Vegetable margarine (shortening)	13g	25g	38g	50g
	(½oz/1 tbsp)	(1oz/2 tbsp)	(1½oz/¼ cup)	(1¾oz/¼ cup)
Soya milk	13ml	25ml	38ml	50ml
	(1 tbsp)	(2 tbsp)	(3 tbsp)	(3 tbsp)
Icing (confectioners') sugar	45g	90g	135g	175g
	(1¾oz/½ cup)	(3¼oz/¾ cup)	(5oz/1 cup)	(6oz/1¼ cups)

Diabetic sponge cake

It is strongly recommended that you divide this cake mixture into two lined tins (pans) of equal size to achieve the baking times in the chart overleaf. If you have only one tin, halve the mixture and cook one half at a time. It is also important to remember to use only diabetic jam (jelly) and cream filling (see recipe page 149) in this sponge cake; the sugar content in ordinary jam and buttercream recipes is far too high for diabetics.

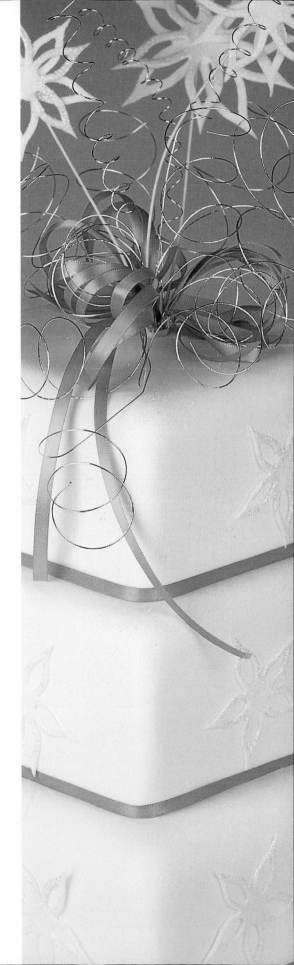

Diabetic sponge cake

Round/square cakes				
Round	13cm	15cm	18cm	20cm
	(5in)	(6in)	(7in)	(8in)
Square	10cm	13cm	15cm	18cm
	(4in)	(5in)	(6in)	(7in)
Low-fat margarine	85g	175g	265g	350g
	(3oz/½ cup)	(6oz/¾ cup)	(9½oz/1¼ cups)	(12oz/1½cups)
Caster (superfine) sugar/	40g	75g	115g	150g
sugar substitute	(1½oz/¼cup)	(2¾oz/¼ cup)	(4oz/½ cup)	(5½oz/1¼ cups)
Eggs	2	3	4–5	6
Self-raising (self-rising)	85g	175g	265g	350g
flour	(3oz/⅔ cup)	(6oz/1½cups)	(9½oz/2¼ cups)	(12oz/3 cups)
Hot water	15–20ml	30–40ml	50–60ml	70–80ml
	(1 tbsp)	(2–3 tbsp)	(3–4 tbsp)	(5 tbsp)
Vanilla essence	to taste	to taste	to taste	to taste
(extract) (optional)				
Approximate baking time at 170°C/350°F/Gas Mark 4				
	20mins	25mins	30mins	40mins

method

1. In a mixing bowl, cream together the low-fat margarine and caster sugar/sugar substitute until the mixture is white and fluffy.

2. Stir in one egg at a time with a little of the self-raising flour, until all of the eggs and flour have been incorporated. Add the hot water and a little vanilla essence, if necessary, to soften the mixture.

3. Divide the mixture equally between two lined tins (pans), then bake immediately.

Diabetic cream filling

As the artificial sweetener in this recipe has a very strong taste, blend the filling and apply a thin layer to the cake just before it is to be eaten. The flavourings that follow also help to disguise the taste of the artificial sweetener.

Flavourings for diabetic cream filling

COFFEE Add just enough water to 1 teaspoon instant coffee to dissolve it, then mix this into the diabetic cream filling.
CHOCOLATE Blend 2 teaspoons cocoa powder into the diabetic cream filling.

Diabetic cream filling

Round/square cakes				
Round	13cm	15cm	18cm	20cm
	(5in)	(6in)	(7in)	(8in)
Square	10cm	13cm	15cm	18cm
	(4in)	(5in)	(6in)	(7in)
Artificial	30ml	60ml	90ml	120ml
sweetener	(2 tbsp)	(4 tbsp)	(6 tbsp)	(8 tbsp)
Low-fat	25g	50g	75g	120g
margarine	(1oz/	(1¾oz/	(2¾oz/	(4½oz/
	2 tbsp)	¼ cup)	⅓ cup)	½ cup)

Buttercream

The quantities below will give you enough buttercream to fill and cover the tops and sides of your cakes.

Buttercream icing

Round/square cakes				
Round	13cm	15cm	18cm	20cm
	(5in)	(6in)	(7in)	(8in)
Square	10cm	13cm	15cm	18cm
	(4in)	(5in)	(6in)	(7in)
Butter/margarine	60g	125g	180g	250g
	(2¼oz/4 tbsp)	(4½oz/½ cup)	(6oz/¾ cup)	(9oz/1 cup)
Icing (confectioners') sugar	250g	500g	750g	1kg
	(9oz/1¾ cups)	(1lb 2oz/3¼ cups)	(1lb 10oz/5 cups)	(2lb 4oz/7 cups)
Hot water	10ml	20ml	30ml	40ml
	(2 tsp)	(4 tsp)	(2 tbsp)	(2½ tbsp)

method

1. Cream the butter/margarine in a mixing bowl until it is almost white in colour.

2. Stir in the icing sugar a little at a time.

3. Continue stirring in the icing sugar and gradually add the water. (The main purpose of the water in this recipe is to soften the consistency of the buttercream if necessary.)

4. Blend until the buttercream has a smooth, spreading consistency.

5. Use the buttercream immediately or freeze it in a plastic bag or airtight container for up to a month. Give it a thorough stir just before use.

Marzipan

See the marzipan guide on page 140 for the amount of marzipan needed to cover different-sized cakes. The quantities below will give you enough marzipan to cover the tops and sides of your cakes.

Round/square cakes				
Round	13cm	15cm	18cm	20cm
	(5in)	(6in)	(7in)	(8in)
Square	10cm	13cm	15cm	18cm
	(4in)	(5in)	(6in)	(7in)
Ground almonds	115g	225g	350g	450g
	(4oz/¾ cup)	(8oz/1½ cups)	(12oz/2½ cups)	(1lb/3¼ cups)
Icing (confectioners') sugar	55g	115g	175g	225g
	(2oz/½cup)	(4oz/1 cup)	(6oz/1½ cups)	(8oz/2 cups)
Caster (superfine) sugar	55g	115g	175g	225g
	(2oz/¼ cup)	(4oz/½ cup)	(6oz/¾ cup)	(8oz/1 cup)
Egg yolks	2	4	6	8
Rum/brandy (optional)	3ml	5ml	8ml	10ml
	(½ tsp)	(1 tsp)	(1½ tsp)	(2 tsp)

method

1. In a mixing bowl, blend together the ground almonds, icing sugar and caster sugar.

2. Add the egg yolks and the rum or brandy, if used.

3. Knead the mixture – but do not overknead or it will become oily – and use immediately.

Egg-free marzipan

See the marzipan guide on page 140 for the amount of marzipan needed to cover different-sized cakes. The quantities below will give you enough egg-free marzipan to cover the tops and sides of your cakes.

Round/square cakes				
Round	13cm (5in)	15cm (6in)	18cm (7in)	20cm (8in)
Square	10cm (4in)	13cm (5in)	15cm (6in)	18cm (7in)
Icing (confectioners') sugar	250g (9oz/1¾ cups)	500g (1lb 2oz/3¼ cups)	750g (1lb 10oz/5 cups)	1kg (2lb 4oz/7 cups)
Water	125ml (4fl oz/½ cup)	250ml (9fl oz/1 cup)	375ml (13fl oz/1½ cups)	500ml (18fl oz/2¼ cups)
Cream of tartar	pinch	0.5ml (⅛ tsp)	2ml (½ tsp)	2ml (½ tsp)
Ground almonds	75g (2¾oz/½ cup)	125g (4½oz/1 cup)	190g (7oz/1½ cups)	250g (9oz/1¾ cups)
Liquid glucose	15ml (1 tbsp)	22.5ml (1½ tbsp)	30ml (2 tbsp)	30ml (2 tbsp)
Essence (extract) of your choice (optional)	2.5ml (½ tsp)	5ml (1 tsp)	7.5ml (1½ tsp)	10ml (2 tsp)

method

1. Put the icing sugar and water in a pan and dissolve the sugar over a low heat.
2. Once it has dissolved completely, raise the heat to 120°C/250°F until the water boils.
3. Remove the mixture from the heat and leave it to cool for 20 minutes.
4. Add the cream of tartar, ground almonds, liquid glucose and essence, if used, and beat until the mixture is thick and creamy.
5. Leave the mixture to cool completely, then turn it out onto a clean work surface and knead until it is smooth.

Nut-free marzipan

See the marzipan guide on page 140 for the amount of marzipan needed to cover different-sized cakes. The quantities below will give you enough nut-free marzipan to cover the tops and sides of your cakes.

Round/square cakes				
Round	13cm (5in)	15cm (6in)	18cm (7in)	20cm (8in)
Square	10cm (4in)	13cm (5in)	15cm (6in)	18cm (7in)
Icing (confectioners') sugar	250g (9oz/1¾ cups)	500g (1lb 2oz/3¼ cups)	750g (1lb 10oz/5 cups)	1kg (2lb 4oz/7 cups)
Water	125ml (4fl oz/½ cup)	250ml (9fl oz/1 cup)	375ml (13fl oz/1½ cups)	500ml (18fl oz/2¼ cups)
Cream of tartar	pinch	0.5ml (⅛ tsp)	2ml (½ tsp)	2ml (½ tsp)
Ground rice	75g (2¾oz/½ cup)	125g (4½oz/1 cup)	190g (7oz/1½ cups)	250g (9oz/1¾ cups)
Eggs	1	1	2	2
Essence (extract) of your choice (optional)	2.5ml (½ tsp)	5ml (1 tsp)	7.5ml (1½ tsp)	10ml (2 tsp)

method

1. Put the icing sugar and water in a pan and dissolve the sugar over a low heat.
2. Once it has dissolved completely, raise the heat to 120°C/250°F until the water boils.
3. Remove the mixture from the heat and leave it to cool for 20 minutes.
4. Add the cream of tartar, ground rice, egg and essence, if used, and beat the mixture until thick and creamy.
5. Leave the mixture to cool completely, then turn it out onto a clean work surface and knead until it is smooth.

Sugarpaste

See the sugarpaste (rolled fondant or ready-to-roll icing) guide on page 140 for the amount of sugarpaste needed to cover different-sized cakes. The quantities given below will give you enough sugarpaste to cover the tops and sides of your cakes.

Sugarpaste

Round/square cakes				
Round	13cm	15cm	18cm	20cm
	(5in)	(6in)	(7in)	(8in)
Square	10cm	13cm	15cm	18cm
	(4in)	(5in)	(6in)	(7in)
Icing (confectioners') sugar	450g	450g	900g	900g
	(1lb/3¼ cups)	(1lb/3¼ cups)	(2lb/6½ cups)	(2lb/6½ cups)
Rose water, lemon juice or kirsch (optional)	to taste	to taste	to taste	to taste
Water	5ml	30ml	45ml	60ml
	(1 tsp)	(2 tbsp)	(3 tbsp)	(4 tbsp)
Powdered gelatine	2 tsp	4 tsp	6 tsp	8 tsp
Liquid glucose	5ml	10ml	15ml	20ml
	(1 tsp)	(2 tsp)	(3 tsp)	(4 tsp)

method

1. Sieve the icing sugar into a large mixing bowl. Stir in the rose water, lemon juice or kirsch, if used.
2. Spoon the water into a separate bowl or saucepan. Sprinkle over the powdered gelatine and leave it to "sponge" in the water.
3. Gently heat the gelatine mixture in the microwave or over the hob (stove), but do not allow it to boil. Stir in the liquid glucose.
4. Stir most of the icing sugar into the gelatine mixture one spoonful at a time. When it begins to stiffen, knead in the remaining icing sugar. You may find it is easier to turn out the mixture onto a work surface before you do this.
5. Put the mixture in a plastic bag and remove all of the air. Leave it for 24 hours before use, and use it within two weeks. There is no need to refrigerate sugarpaste; simply give it a good knead before use.

Royal icing

The following quantities will give you enough royal icing to cover the tops and sides of your cakes.

Round/square cakes				
Round	13cm	15cm	18cm	20cm
	(5in)	(6in)	(7in)	(8in)
Square	10cm	13cm	15cm	18cm
	(4in)	(5in)	(6in)	(7in)
Egg whites (albumen)	1	2	3	4
Icing (confectioners') sugar	250g	500g	750g	1kg
	(9oz/1¾ cups)	(1lb 2oz/3¼ cups)	(1lb 10oz/5 cups)	(2lb 4oz/7 cups)
Glycerine (optional)	2.5ml	5ml	7.5ml	10ml
	(½ tsp)	(1 tsp)	(1½ tsp)	(2 tsp)

method

1. Place the egg whites in a bowl and beat, adding most of the icing sugar a spoonful at a time.
2. Add the glycerine, if used.
3. Continue beating in the icing sugar until you have achieved the right consistency.
4. Store the royal icing in an airtight container for up to a week. To get the best results, stir it once a day and then again just before use. There is no need to refrigerate royal icing.

Royal icing with albumen substitute

The quantities below will give you enough egg-free royal icing to cover the tops and sides of your cakes.

Round/square cakes				
Round	13cm	15cm	18cm	20cm
	(5in)	(6in)	(7in)	(8in)
Square	10cm	13cm	15cm	18cm
	(4in)	(5in)	(6in)	(7in)
Albumen substitute	7.5g	15g	22g	30g
	(¼oz/1 tbsp)	(½oz/2 tbsp)	(1oz/¼ cup)	(1¼oz/¼ cup)
Water	37ml	75ml	115ml	150ml
	(3 tbsp)	(5 tbsp)	(8 tbsp)	(5fl oz)
Icing (confectioners') sugar	250g	500g	750g	1kg
	(9oz/1¾ cups)	(1lb 2oz/3¼ cups)	(1lb 10oz/5 cups)	(2lb 4oz/7 cups)
Glycerine (optional)	2.5ml	5ml	7.5ml	10ml
	(½ tsp)	(1 tsp)	(1½ tsp)	(2 tsp)

method

1. In a mixing bowl, blend the albumen substitute and the water.

2. Once the albumen substitute has dissolved completely, strain the mixture through a very fine sieve.

3. Add the icing sugar a spoonful at a time until you have achieved the consistency that you want.

4. Blend in the glycerine, if used.

Mexican paste

If you are pressed for time, you can buy ready-made Mexican paste. Preparing your own is not difficult – indeed, the only hitch is that you need to make it 24 hours before use.

The recipe below gives 1kg (2lb 4oz) of Mexican paste. If this is more than you need, cut it into small blocks, wrap these in cling film (plastic wrap) and a plastic bag, and put them in the freezer until required.

250g (9oz/1¾ cups) icing (confectioners') sugar

15ml (1 tbsp) gum tragacanth or Tylo powder

5ml (1 tsp) liquid glucose

30ml (2 tbsp) cold water

method

1. Stir together the icing sugar and gum tragacanth/Tylo powder in a mixing bowl.

2. Make a small well in the centre of the mixture and add the liquid glucose.

3. Add the water 5ml (1 tsp) at a time, all the while mixing by hand or at a slow speed.

4. Continue adding water and stirring until the paste is thoroughly blended.

5. Wrap the mixture in cling film and a plastic bag, and leave it in the refrigerator for 24 hours before use.

Flower paste

5 tsp cold water
2 tsp powdered gelatine
450g (1lb/3½ cups) icing
   (confectioners') sugar
3 tsp gum tragacanth
2 tsp cornflour (cornstarch)
2 tsp liquid glucose
2 tsp white vegetable fat
   (vegetable shortening)
1 large egg white (a large egg is about
   68g/2¼oz) (or an equivalent quantity
   of mixed powdered albumen)

method

1. Measure the cold water into the microwave-proof bowl and sprinkle the gelatine over the surface. Leave to stand for a few minutes.
2. Sift the icing sugar into the bowl of a heavy-duty mixer (this must be microwave-proof – if your bowl is metal use a Pyrex bowl, then tip into the mixer bowl after heating). Sprinkle in the gum tragacanth and cornflour, and microwave on half power for 1–1½ minutes.
3. Microwave the gelatine for a few seconds (try 10-second bursts and stir between each) on half power until just dissolved, then add the glucose and vegetable fat. Stir well until all is dissolved, if necessary returning the bowl to the microwave for a few more seconds. Do not overheat.
4. Make a well in the centre of the icing sugar and pour in the gelatine mixture. Add the egg white.
5. Heat the beater of the mixer in hot water and dry. Beat the ingredients together on slow speed until all ingredients are combined. The paste will be a dull beige at this stage.
6. Turn the mixer to the maximum and, keeping your arm on the mixer's arm for stability, beat until the paste is white and stringy (about 5 minutes).
7. Place the completed paste in a plastic bag inside an airtight container and refrigerate.
8. Leave to mature overnight before using. To keep for longer periods, divide into small amounts and freeze.

Chocolate moulding icing

200g (7oz) chocolate
65ml (⅓ cup) liquid glucose

method

Melt the chocolate over hot water in a bowl and warm the liquid glucose. Mix in the liquid glucose to form a paste; keep mixing until it comes away from the side of the bowl and you can form it into a ball. Place it in a plastic bag and leave at room temperature overnight before use. To use this paste, knead the mixture until it is pliable. You can heat in the microwave to soften, but do not heat for any longer than 5 seconds or it will be ruined. To store, keep in a cool, dry place in an airtight container for up to 2 months.

Piping chocolate

40g (1½oz) chocolate
5ml (1 tsp) glycerine

method

Melt the chocolate as you did for the moulding icing and stir in the glycerine. Put the mix into your piping (decorating) bag and use immediately.

Pastillage

15g (½oz) gelatine powder
60ml (4 tbsp) water
30ml (2 tbsp) liquid glucose
450g (1lb/3½ cups) icing
   (confectioners') sugar
a little cornflour (cornstarch)

method

Sprinkle the gelatine over the water and leave to dissolve for 5 minutes or so. Either heat in the microwave or stand the bowl over hot water until the gelatine has dissolved. Add the liquid glucose – if you warm your spoon first, you will find the glucose will slide off easily. Mix the icing sugar into the liquid and add only a little cornflour to form the dough. Cornflour dries the paste out, so keep it to the minimum. This paste is excellent to work; it can be frozen if you do not need it all at once.

Templates

ABCDEFG
HIJKLMN
OPQRSTU
VWXYZ

abcdefghij
klmnopqrst
uvwxyz?.

1234567890

ABCDEFGHIJKLMN
OPQRSTUVWXYZ123
4567890?!

Templates for lace work

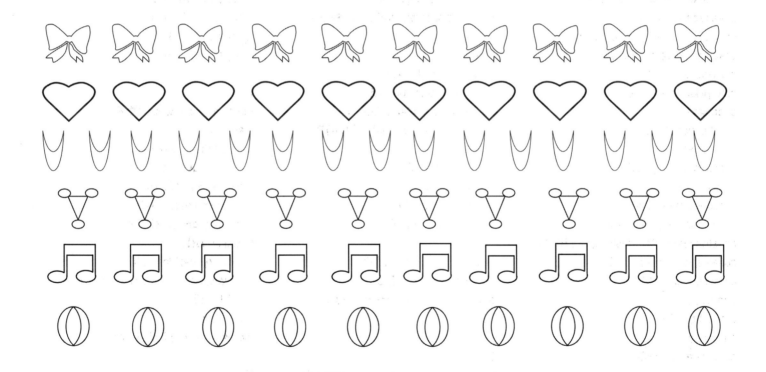

Index

H. 3/08

W 9/08